From Shoeshine to Star Wars
The chronicles of Walt Jourdan

Walt Jourdan and Lee Jourdan

Library of Congress Control number: 2016918742

ISBN-13: 978-1537535685
ISBN-10: 1537535684

For Dad, who taught me to care for others.
For Mom, and her undying love.
For Ruby, who always believed in me.
~ Walt Jourdan

For my wife, Diane. My rock. My Inspiration.
~ Lee Jourdan

CONTENTS

Forewords   Pg 5

1   Shoeshine Boy   Pg 12

2   Origins   Pg 23

3   Hustler   Pg 28

4   Enforcer   Pg 42

5   Mom   Pg 50

6   High School   Pg 55

7   College   Pg 62

8   Navy   Pg 78

9   Ruby   Pg 98

10 Vocation   Pg 118

11 Broken   Pg 127

12 Star Wars   Pg 143

13 Epilogue   Pg 156

FOREWORD BY RANDALL CUNNINGHAM

Walter "Pop" Jourdan has been a faithful member of our congregation for about a decade. I knew that we had a kindred spirit when he began sharing football stories with me from his college career. Pop is a man's man. And I know that he would have been one tough customer on the gridiron. But it was his intestinal fortitude that was on full display when I went to visit him in the hospital as he waged the fight of his life battling lymphoma. Despite his age, he fought back with the courage, grace and dignity that have come to define this brother.

It has been a family affair with the Jourdan's. His granddaughter and his eldest daughter-in-law have danced on the praise dance team, and his eldest son has been the guitarist on the worship team for ten years. And my wife and his eldest granddaughter have formed a special bond. But I think the thing that I am most proud of is the fact that Pop came to accept Jesus as his Lord and Savior at our church, Remnant Ministries. As Senior Pastor, this commitment is of eternal importance to me.

Pop is a story teller. And it doesn't seem to matter what the current topic is, he is always ready to produce an anecdotal muse that seems to magically transport you back to that precise moment where he provides you with a first party perspective. He has always had a passion for the welfare of our youth, and he has shared plenty of stories about his many years as a Pop Warner football coach. It was not just about the winnings and the championships, of which there were plenty, but more importantly it was about the life preparation that it afforded those kids that he was most proud of. He related to me the colorful and creative stories, and perhaps minor exaggerations concerning their opposition, that he would foist upon his players to get them fired up for the game. He once shared how he told his boys that the middle linebacker from this week's rivals liked to try and plant a kiss on you once he had you down in the dog pile. He said that the team played with a whole new vigor that week and did all they could to avoid any prolonged contact during the game! That's Pop.

Whatever it took to motivate his team, he was all about results.

This book has been skillfully crafted by his son, Lee, to provide you a front row seat so that you too can witness first-hand the amazing experiences of this unique individual. God has blessed him with a long and productive life, full of giving and compassion, as well as the capacity to recall, relate and frame those experiences in manner that are both inspiring and relatable to all that have had the good fortune to spend time in his company.

August 2016
Randall Cunningham
Senior Pastor
Remnant Ministries, Las Vegas NV
NFL MVP 1990, 1998

FOREWORD BY SUSAN TOLER CARR

I have known Walt Jourdan all my life. My father, Burl Toler, was his college team mate, roommate and, most importantly, a lifelong present and compassionate family friend. Collectively, my siblings and I have always affectionately referred to him as: "Uncle Walt."

Uncle Walt has the gift of gab. I have witnessed, many times during our frequent conversations, the depth of his exceptional memory. He has shared details of many happenings from over 65 years ago. I was dumbfounded when he told me vivid stories about his college days with my dad – even when he informed me that my father's major in college was engineering. As a professional engineer myself, I never knew the minute backstory of my dad's post-secondary academic accomplishments. However, he was known throughout the city of San Francisco as a man of integrity, a great educator, and that weekend NFL official who was often spotted on television running up and down the field. One day, when I was going through my dad's 1951 college duffle bag, I spotted engineering worksheets. The color and style of the workbooks were exactly how Uncle Walt had previously described. Amazing.

Another funny visual was when Uncle Walt dramatically staged (with enthusiasm) how he and my dad once had to improvise to mitigate the chill of the night. Using his hands as props he motioned the layout of the minimal "dorm room" (aka former officer's quarters) furnishings, that included a steam heater that turned off at 10:00 PM. He then described how he dressed himself in jeans, a sweatshirt, and a camel-hair coat, and stole the blankets from my father's bed to keep from freezing. When my father returned, they huddled together to stay warm. He emphatically told me: "We had to sleep like that for that one moment in time literally to stay alive because it was so frigid!"

So, as I read *From Shoeshine to Star Wars,* the descriptive and enthralling words popped off the pages. I really did not want to put the book down. Between the lines, my mind traveled with Uncle Walt through the yesteryears, historical events, and the challenges of the times. I was right there with him – that fly on the wall each time as he used his talent and quick-witted spirit to shine shoes, interact with relatives, teachers and friends, attend school, lift weights, play football, enlist in the navy, raise his family or work a job.

When he had shortcomings or doors that closed in his face, he often felt like that fly in a bowl of milk. Alone. But he did not give up. His family and village supported him along the way. And his persistence was because of his humble beginnings, and the education he garnered from the streets and in the classroom – they were all his training grounds. His muscles bulged and his mind got stronger. He went through many trials and tribulations. He transitioned from being Colored, to Negro, to Black, and now he continues to stand tall as a proud African American.

Collectively, the encounters throughout his life made it possible for him to gain the resilience, grit, and determination he needed to be successful. When he fell down – he got back up. He thrived. He was resourceful. His eyes were on the prize.

It is a true gift to the readers that he managed to tuck pertinent details in the diary of his head and present his life in print for others like me to appreciate. I am so forever grateful that I got a snapshot of the life of this talented man, my Uncle Walt. This young shoeshiner and star wars contributor finally got his seat at the table in that infamous house at 1600 Pennsylvania Avenue. You will have to read this book to find out what I mean. And I guarantee you will not be disappointed.

August 2016
Susan Toler Carr

1 SHOESHINE

In as much as the Great Depression altered life in 1937, it did nothing to delay the rise of the sun. It peered through the curtains and painted long strips of white light on the plaster wall, which only served as a reminder of the long, fresh welts on my butt and the back of my legs. I wondered how I would make any money that day. To make money, I had to walk. And I wasn't sure I could. I had slept on my stomach all night because the welts made it impossible for me to sleep on my back. If I moved – even the slightest – my skin felt like it was on fire. It felt as though the leather strap was leaping on me again, as it had the night before. The strap smelled of shoe leather, a smell I was well familiar with. But it was more pungent, because it was mixed with the sweat from Little Walt. That was me.

My brother, Bobby, three and a half years my junior, lay next to me in the "Do-fold." He was sprawled out, deep in his slumber, as only six-year-olds can do. The fold out bed we slept in, in the family room, was converted back to a couch during the day. I once asked my Uncle Spencer why it was called a Do-fold. "Because it do fold!", he said,

Bobby would sometimes be a victim of collateral damage. Dad would come home from work, get a briefing of the transgressions I had committed, whip the blankets off us and get a couple of good lashes in before I could mount any kind of wiggly defense. The result was that Bobby would catch a few blows as well. This didn't happen every night of course, and Dad took no pleasure in the task. But he did what had to be done.

That night was different because Dad was home early enough to dole out discipline before I was asleep. After the briefing from Mom, he bellowed, "Mister!" And the shrill in my spine found its familiar place.

When most kids got into trouble, their parents yelled their full, proper name. But not Dad. He just growled, "Mister!" And I knew an ass whuppin' was comin'. And it came by way of me assuming "The Position."

There were to be many firsts in my life, but this was not one of them. My brothers and sisters came to know The Position too, but I knew it best. I was more adventurous than my siblings, and those adventures took me well out of earshot of my mother, Jennie, worrying her for hours at a time.

I had returned from an all-day adventure of playing Huckleberry Finn, with my Japanese-American friends, Harry and Henry Mizote. Harry and Henry could be gone all day, and their mother would have no idea where they were, but they never got into trouble. I don't know if it was because their parents didn't know what kind of trouble was lurking for young boys exploring miles from their homes, or if they felt that the adventures were just part of growing up, but for Harry and Henry, there were no consequences for disappearing all day. Unfortunately, just being of Japanese descent would soon be consequence enough.

I snuck slowly up to the house so as not to alert Mom. Chances were that Bobby had already ratted me out anyway, as revenge for not taking him along. But there was no way to know for sure. As I stealthily approached the house, I saw my neighborhood friends playing marbles in the dirt outside the kitchen window. That's when I knew I was in trouble. My friends could play marbles anywhere, but they were parked at my house. They weren't so much interested in the game as they were in the entertainment that would be provided by my ass whuppin'. Nothin' like hearing the wails of your buddy as he got a whuppin'. And oh, what wails I would deliver.

I still had to do everything I could to avoid the inevitable. Before joining the marble game, I rubbed dirt into the knees of my pants to make my mom think I had been there all along. That didn't work, of course. As soon as she heard my voice, she stormed out of the house, whipping me up by my arm as I pleaded for leniency. Spankings from my mother were nothing. But I screamed and cried in the hope of generating enough sympathy that she wouldn't tell my dad when he got home. That didn't work either. That's why Dad would put me in The Position.

Everyone called Dad "Big Walt." He wasn't called Big Walt to differentiate himself from Little Walt. Big Walt was always big. He stood 5'10" and weighed 240 lbs. That was the size of offensive linemen in those days. He had put that heft to good use working as a cement finisher for my grandfather in New Orleans before he moved to Oakland for good in 1930. Dad could lift one 94-pound bag of cement with one hand and throw it in to the cement hopper. He had a chest resembling half a whiskey barrel and shoulders carved from granite. His arms were thick and muscular.

To assume The Position, I had to be naked and bent over at the waist. Dad would wedge my head between his powerful legs, gripping my neck with his knees. My arms were wrapped around his legs. My wrists held together, clamped by one of his huge, powerful hands. My raw, naked butt was accessible to the 4-inch wide leather razor strap held by his other hand. There wasn't much butt on this skinny nine-year-old, but what was there danced and wiggled in an attempt to dodge the descending strap. But the powerful legs that held my head and the strong hand that gripped my wrists, made sure that the strap found its mark again, and again, and again. It left long welts that lasted for days. No, it was best to sleep on my stomach, if I was to get any sleep at all.

But it was Saturday, and the sun was lengthening those strips of sunshine on the wall, willing me to rise. It was a workday after all. Sure, occasionally I would tote my shoeshine box to the bars on a weekday after school – I could always find some customers looking to impress the ladies with a quick shine. But Saturday is when the big money could be made. The nation was still in the midst of the Great Depression. Daily wages at US Steel had risen to $5, but if I hustled, I could make $10, $12, sometimes $14 by the time I had finished my rounds.

Mom was dependent on me to do my part. I loved the look on her face when I pulled off my shoe and extracted the slightly damp, neatly folded dollar bills that I had traded my coins for at the weigh station. On the way home, I would stop by the Santa Fe Station lumber yard in search of a piece of lumber with a nail protruding from it. A bag of coins on an unarmed boy was like the sweet smell of dead flesh to a vulture. The older kids just outside my neighborhood knew I had been out hustling all day and would love to relieve me of my hard earned cash before I made it home. It was wise to change those coins into dollar bills, and to have some protection.

But first I had to make the money, and that meant forcing myself out of bed. It always helped to envision my route. I gathered the tools of my trade: my shoe shine box that I had cut, hammered, and constructed - brown and black wax, a brush, and rag. But not just any rag. I had gone down to the pool hall, and happened to catch the pool hall man in the right mood, which wasn't always the case. He gave me some old felt from the pool tables. That was the best cloth. It was strong and smooth. You could almost see yourself in the shine after a polish with that cloth. I also carried my stack of *Look* and *Liberty* magazines. I sold those for five cents each. And boy could I sell. I had that gift. I sold so many magazines those days that the regional distributor made my house the drop off point for the whole neighborhood. I made an extra half cent for each magazine the other kids in the neighborhood sold too. Multi-level marketing before multi-level marketing was cool.

The third way to make money was to dance. Some of my best customers could be found in bars. Occasionally, one of them would drop a coin in the juke box and tell me to dance, and then throw me a few pennies for doing so. They loved to watch the little Colored boy dance, and would make their comments. I didn't like it. It was demeaning, even at that young age, but I could earn some pennies, so I would put on my grin and my best moves. From time to time, I could get revenge on some of the real mean ones, the ones I didn't think I would see again real soon. If they would call me nigger, or rub my head for "luck," I would put black shoe polish on their brown shoes. They wouldn't notice until they left the dark bar, or maybe not even until the next day. By the time I saw them again, if they mentioned anything, I would say it was my buddy, Wesley Randolph. Heck, we all looked alike to them anyway.

I always took the same route when I worked on a Saturday. I had lots of regular customers, White and Colored, which treated me well. My route started at San Pablo and 34th Street. From there I would turn right, and walk nineteen blocks to 14th street, stopping in all of the bars and other businesses along the way- peddling magazines and shoe shines. City Hall was on 14th Street, and the press room was inside. Lots of opportunity there. Then I would make my way to 521 14th Street to attend to my regular shoeshine customers at The Meniketti Accordion Studio. The Meniketti studio was a staple in the Oakland Area. Mr. Meniketti would go on to open up another, larger studio further north, and the family would build a legacy of music in Oakland. The most successful of the family would be Dave Meniketti, the legendary guitarist with the rock group Y&T. He would go on to tour with Ozzy Osbourne, Peter Frampton, and White Snake.

After Meniketti's, I continued east then walk south all the way to the foot of Broadway, where Jack London Square would eventually be built. Then I would retrace my steps back up Broadway to 13th Street, turn right, go one block to the Oakland Tribune paper building and pick up a few more shines. Turn north and go to 22nd Street (since renamed West Grand) to the bowling alley looking for business. Then turn north and go all the way out to 55th Street, with more bars and family owned businesses along the way. 55th Street was as far as I would go north before working my way through Emeryville, which was full of card rooms (draw poker was legal there at the time), and then head home. All told, I would walk about 10 miles and shine 50 to 60 pairs of shoes.

There were no African Americans in Oakland in 1937. There were no Blacks, there weren't even any Negros. But there were plenty of Colored People, or Creole if you were from Louisiana. And that's where Big Walt was from.

This was one man that could not be defined by his appearance. When he finished eighth grade, he hit a crossroad – finish school, or drop out like his brother Spencer and work to help his family. Dad quit school. Spencer and Dad became well-known businessmen around the city of Oakland. At their peak, Dad and Uncle Spencer owned a number of businesses including a boarding house, barber shop, gambling house, cab company, gas station, a baseball team, a used car lot, and a lumber mill. They also had leadership positions in the only labor union for Colored workers in the West Coast Shipyards. Called Boilermakers A-26, the union was the result of a trip that Uncle Spencer had taken to Kansas City. He was the secretary and treasurer, providing day to day leadership of the union. Dad was the inspector and dispatcher. I didn't know it at the time, but this resourcefulness - this willingness to take on new commerce, to take on any job to make ends meet - became part of me. I would need to draw on that reserve in dark times.

My dad was a disciplinarian. You had to be if you were going to be a father to sixteen children. Dad fathered a total of eleven of them himself, including Laura and Walter who were stillborn. The other five were part of the deal when he married their mothers. He would dole out the whippings and then hug you and tell you how much he loved you. He fathered five of the children with his first wife, my mother Jennie, and then six more with Menomonee after Jennie passed. Herman, Myrtle, Laura, Walter, Georgiana, Alges, Walter (Little Walt), Bobby, Laurie, Jimmy, Howell (Dutchie), John-John, Toni, Brenda, Spencer, and David. I was the first child fathered by my dad that wasn't still born. So I had his name.

For each day I woke up sore from a whuppin' the night before, there were hundreds more when I awoke with the anticipation of a fun filled day with my father. We had picnics and trips to the fair. And when the Negro baseball teams barnstormed into town, he would whisk me away in the car and we would find our spot in the bleachers.

But none of those trips were as exciting as the one just he and I went on to the 16th Street train station to get a glimpse of the man in the stingy-brim hat. It was July 14, 1939. The great man was in the Bay Area for a tour of the newly finished bridges, and to visit the site of the 1939 Golden Gate Exposition. He had stopped in Oakland on the train to shake hands and kiss babies. The whole town knew he was coming, and it looked like the whole town had turned out to greet him. The streets were packed from curb to storefront. We were far in the back, so Dad hoisted me up on his shoulders to get a peek. President Franklin D. Roosevelt waved to the crowd from his convertible. I'm sure he never looked right at me, but I waved back all the same. I'm sure dad thought I would never have a chance to see a US president again, and I would never get any closer than I was on that day. He was wrong on both counts.

2 ORIGINS

In the late 1800s, a Frenchman from Virginia, with the family name of Jourdan, fell in love with a woman of African and Choctaw Indian descent and they were married. They migrated to Grand Isle, Louisiana where many French descendants had settled. They had fourteen children, one of which was Walter David Jourdan. Walter David Jourdan was my paternal grandfather.

In the mid to late 1860s, Edmund McIlhenny, a food lover and avid gardener, was given seeds of *Capsicum frutescence* peppers from Central America. He sowed the seeds on Avery Island in South Louisiana, nurtured the plants, and created what became known as Tabasco sauce. Robert Thomas, a slave who worked on the McIlhenny plantation, had a daughter named Georgianna. Georgianna Thomas was my paternal grandmother. Anyone who knows me knows that I love to spice my food with Tabasco sauce. I suppose it's in my blood.

Grand Isle, where my grandfather had settled, was known for annual floods, and by 1893 the Jourdans had had enough of the floods and relocated their family to New Orleans. Walter David Jourdan met and married Georgianna Thomas in New Orleans. They had several children, one of them was Walter Thomas Jourdan, my father, Big Walt - born to them on February 28, 1902.

My father had an older sister named Rose. She was married to a man named John Banks, Sr. In the early 1900s, John and Rose migrated to California looking for work. In 1910 they sent for my grandmother who took two of her sons, Spencer and Walter.

My dad came back to New Orleans around 1920 to help grandpa with his cement business. That's when he met my mother, Jennie. After arriving in New Orleans, Dad got in to an altercation with a knife wielding attacker. Grandpa stepped in to protect his son and took the knife in the stomach. A Colored man with a knife wound did not generate much sympathy in Louisiana in the 1920s. He was patched up and sent on his way. The internal stitching was tenuous at best and severely affected his digestion. The prognosis called for an enema. Nothing more. Grandpa protested that the enema was too hot, scalding him internally. He was admonished by the White nurse with a terse "Shut up, nigger," and the enema continued. Between the botched surgery and the scalding enema, internal bleeding ensued which led to grandpa's death shortly thereafter. Of course, there was no autopsy performed, certainly not for a Colored man. Grandpa died in 1925, three years before I was born. But Dad honored him by giving me his full name: Walter David Jourdan. I would continue the tradition, naming my first son Walter David Jourdan, Jr.

I am told that I created the fanfare for my birth that goes down in the annals of Jourdan history as my first act of defiance. They say that Great Uncle Darius, who was present at the birth, bounded out of the house like an untethered stallion. His voice echoed off the sky and ricocheted into the streets, announcing that he had a brand new nephew and, "He ain't afraid of White folks!" Because the first thing that nephew did was send a warm stream of pee right in to the White doctor's face

I was born to Walter and Jennie Jourdan at 4820 Coliseum Street, North New Orleans, December 19, 1928. I know my parents breathed a sigh of relief when they heard that first wail since the first Little Walt was born without a heartbeat. Stillborn deaths were not recorded in 1928, but of all the deaths that were recorded in 1928, 10% of them were babies who died before their first birthday. If you were Colored, which included Native Americans, Japanese, and Chinese, that number jumped to 14%. In 1928, as a Colored newborn, you only had a one in seven chance of living to see your first birthday. In 2017, God willing, I will celebrate my eighty-ninth.

* * *

In 1884, a decade before the Jourdans moved from Grand Isle to New Orleans, the Southern Pacific Railroad began running the *Sunset Limited* from New Orleans to San Francisco via Los Angeles. It was the first named train in the United States. It could travel from New Orleans to San Francisco in seventy-two hours. The Sunset Limited was Southern Pacific's premier train. Initially, it was an all-Pullman train, which meant it had sleeping cars, but no coaches or regular seats. By 1926, it had added coach seating. The good news was that there was a Pullman car for Coloreds too. The bad news was that it was located right behind the coal car, filling the car with soot and smoke.

But it was still a ride west. So in October 1930, just before my second birthday, Dad carried all of our life's belongings onto the Sunset Limited, with me toddling right behind.

A bumpy seventy-two-hour train trip was a long journey for a toddler. But Dad had moonlighted as a moonshiner in New Orleans and brought along a gallon of the Jourdan blend which, I'm told, he administered to me along the way to keep me calm. In those days, you learned to fend for yourself – more so if you were Colored, because you were not allowed in the dining car. Dad would have to hustle to feed himself and his toddler. Fortunately, a handsome man and his round faced baby boy, traveling alone, were a soft touch for the ladies who happened to have prepared fried chicken, catfish, buttermilk biscuits, potatoes, and lima beans for the long trip. The ladies also wrongly believed that Dad was associated with a well-known preacher with the same last name from Houston. A suggestion that Dad did not feel obligated to deny. We ate well.

My mom and my sister, Georgianna, arrived five months later in February 1931. Soon after their arrival, Georgianna contracted pneumonia. She was not one of the unfortunate 14% that died before their first birthday, but she was unable to recover and passed before her second.

3 HUSTLER

Upon arrival in Oakland, we moved in with Uncle Spencer and his wife, Aunt 'Stelle, on the north side of 36th St., between Market and West streets. It was a non-White neighborhood, but that didn't mean it was all Black. There was a smattering of Asians: Chinese, Japanese, and Filipinos. Later, we moved to 37th St., where I met Harry and Henry Mizote, my Huckleberry Finn friends, and Raymond Gutierrez, who was born in Oakland but whose father was from the Philippines and whose mother was Black. I can remember playing with them as early as when I was four years old, and we remained friends all the way in to junior high school. A friendship that would be interrupted by world events.

When I turned six, I attended Longfellow Grammar School, which became a family tradition.

My whole family attended Longfellow, starting with my oldest cousin, John Banks.

Harry, Henry, Raymond and I galloped to our favorite spots with the carefree spirit of boys who would live forever. Oblivious to how poor we were, we made our own adventures. The pain from the ass whuppin's wasn't enough to quiet the call for our escapades. Equipment temporarily abandoned at construction sites became our playground. Locomotives still warm from a day's work needed to be scaled. We manufactured souvenirs from the locomotives that hadn't shut down for the day by putting construction nails on the tracks, then we ran off and watched them be flattened by the passing train wheels.

It's a wonder we were not maimed or killed while playing around some of that equipment. I guess God had more for us to do.

One day we were deeply entrenched in our own play world of marbles, or hopscotch, when the local hotel handyman eased up to us.

"Hey", pulling some coins out of his pocket, "look what I found in the field by the corner store". We looked at him, then at each other. "There's probably more out there, but the grass and weeds are too high, and I don't have time to do all of that cutting".

Without another word, we stopped what we were doing and sprinted home to grab rakes and hoes. For the next hour we hacked and raked, the better to find the hidden treasure. And sure enough, we were rewarded. A penny here, a nickel there. Just enough to keep us interested - just enough to motivate us to work the whole field. It didn't bother us that, as we left, he came in behind us to bag up the weeds and grass.

When you don't have a lot of money, you don't dwell on it. You just make do. We were masters at creating our own fun. None more creative than me, I thought. We could all make a sling shot, or rubber band gun, or scooter from an old pair of skates. But I often felt the need to do something a bit more.

One day we were playing in the marsh, pretending to be pirates wielding the long cattails as swords when an idea struck me. The velvety cylindrical end of the cattail looked less like the end of a sword, and more like the top of a torch. The idea crystallized in my mind as I uprooted the longest one I could find, and sprinted home to complete my project.

It was easy enough to unscrew the gas cap off of Dad's car. The "hot dog" looking velvety end of the cattail drank in the gasoline as though it was always meant to be. Match boxes were plentiful, because everyone smoked in those days. So when I lit the end and the cattail burst into flames, I held in my hand a more magnificent torch than I could have imagined. I held it high over my head as I marched down the street. All of the kids fell in behind me and I was the drum major in the parade! The hero marching home from war. The conqueror returning with spoils. I was king! Strutting down the street as the gasoline soaked reed billowed fire and black smoke a few feet from my head.

I don't know when Dad saw me, or where he was when he did. All I know is that he swept down on me like an eagle snatching its prey, dragging me off to do what eagles do. It was the worst whuppin' I ever received. And I remember it like it was yesterday.

***

Being a baby of the Great Depression, it was really all I knew. But we knew the difference between the haves and the have-nots. The chasm between the two was widening, and it felt like we were somewhere in the middle. The Great Depression had cast a long, cold shadow on everyone and everything. When I started working as a shoeshine boy, I saw all walks of life. I could tell by the quality of their shoes who was doing well, and who was not. The sole was a window to the soul. Dad was a cement finisher by day, so he was a skilled laborer and pulled in $85 per month, whereas the unskilled laborers made only about $60 per month – if they could find work. At night, before he owned his own gambling house, he dealt cards at a gambling house owned by Mr. Sam Sewell, and later owned by Boss Smith. I don't know how much Dad made working for Sam Sewell, but I know he was always busy. When I got older, in my early teens, I started running numbers for Boss Smith. As sinister as the movies make numbers running sound, it was really just a lottery. An illegal lottery, but a lottery nonetheless. People continued to gamble, even in hard times, because it still gave them hope.

My job as a numbers runner was to run the tickets from the gambling house over to where the Chinese marked the tickets, and then I ran them back to the gambling house. The winning number for the day was based on a well-known formula that included sports scores or stock closings, which were posted in the local paper. People trusted the outcome because the formula and all of the inputs to the formula were known to the public. The reason the government made this business illegal was not for ethical reasons, it was because they couldn't figure out how to get their cut of winnings. It was impossible to tax. These days, lotteries have been legitimized and winnings are taxed, so the government is happy to let people do all of the lottery betting they want.

I learned lessons in school, but what I learned on the streets was equally important. The message was simple: those who worked hard were better off than those who didn't. There were lots of people making money in lots of different ways. The impression these entrepreneurs left on me was the basis for how I would think as an adult. You didn't see a lot of people looking for handouts. You saw people doing what they had to in order to put food on the table.

There were subtle levels of difference among those who broke the law. Dad and Uncle Spencer had no problem with poker, for example, but they wouldn't run a dice game at their gambling house. Their gambling house was frequented by men with colorful names like Biscuits, Nickel Sam, Playboy, Double-Bottom Tex, Red Sweater, Bad Acting Dad, and Railhead. I never knew their real names. No matter how much they would argue, they kept their switch-blades tucked in to their shoes. I was never witness to a situation where they felt they had to extract them. When I was older I learned to hide my switch blade in my shoe too. If only I had learned to just leave it there as well.

Dad and Uncle Spencer didn't run the local brothel, it was behind Boss Smith's gambling house – five houses down the alley from where we lived. The oldest profession in the world was run under the stern eye of Miss Neesie, the madam. Miss Neesie would give the clientele the once over, and collect the money before any services were provided. If you wanted the standard service, you asked for a 5 and 2: $5 for the trick and $2 for the room. I ran errands for the working girls – buying them hamburgers and sodas and such – so I was in and out of the brothel well in to my teens. For a young man transitioning into puberty, seeing half-naked women strutting about was sensory overload, especially a particularly pretty girl, not much older than me, who went by the name of Long Goodie. But Miss Neesie would not allow me to be "mentored" by these learned women. I would have to fumble my way through those lessons with the local girls when the time was right. Little did I know that later, when I grew in to a young man of college age, Long Goodie would notice that I was no longer a boy.

Of course, Dad and Uncle Spencer had to take care of the police. The police all knew where the gambling houses were, and looked the other way if they were properly compensated. The local beat cops could be appeased by slipping them a $20 bill inside of a matchbook. But to make sure he had coverage from the highest levels within the police force, Dad had to make the trip downtown once a month and make the required payments. Some houses didn't compensate like they should and were raided. Dad and Uncle Spencer's place was never bothered.

Although the neighborhood was mostly Colored, Japanese and Chinese businessmen moved in with their family-owned businesses. They set up gambling houses, corner stores, and meat markets. One such establishment, on the west side of Market Street between 36th and 37th streets, was Fong's meat market, established in 1924; the location is still a meat market today.

The most popular Chinese-run business was the Chinese lottery. The Chinese ran lotteries from Mexico to the Canadian border. One such Chinese lottery in our neighborhood was run by Mr. Jack Woo. Mr. Woo was not always timely in his payoffs to local officials, so they often came looking for him. On one such occasion, Mr. Woo came banging on our door, pleading for sanctuary. Dad obliged and hid him in our apartment bathroom. Mr. Woo and my dad became friends, and although Mr. Woo could afford to live outside the Colored neighborhood, he chose to buy a house right next to ours.

Eventually all the Chinese Lotteries were chased out of California, moving to Reno where gambling was legal. Mr. Woo departed with them. In Reno, the major clubs, such as the Harold Club and Harrah's, didn't allow Coloreds to gamble there. A place like the New China Club in Reno, run by the Chinese, was a welcome home to the Colored gambler.

Dad wasn't trying to make criminals out of us; he was just trying to put food on the table. He was clearly involved in illegal activity, but the moment I did anything out of line, out came the razor strap. I understood the difference between what he was doing to make money and what I was doing to get in to mischief. I made no attempt to justify one because of the other. The Jourdan's weren't going to be standing in any bread lines. Even though Dad dropped out of school after the 8th grade, he insisted that we continue to go to school.

The teachers at Longfellow knew all the kids, and were treated with reverence. I respected them all, in particular; Ms. Ardley, Ms. Johnson, Ms. Minnehan, and the principal, Mr. Martin. When you acted up in school, you were sent to the principal's office for punishment. Mr. Roberts, the janitor, held you and the principal would give you an ass whuppin'. Then you got a note for your parents to sign, which they wouldn't sign until after they had given you another whuppin'. I steered clear of any trouble at Longfellow because I respected my teachers.

We had a lot of fun at school, especially with some of the activities we were guided into, like woodworking. I learned to make mallets, bowls for holding and cracking walnuts, and cutting boards for the kitchen. I could draft and construct woodworking projects with the best of them. I really enjoyed doing that. We were also exposed to live theater – where you could meet lots of girls.

Part of me wanted to be a tough kid. The tough

kids – school drop outs – had a cool look about them. But part of me knew I was better than that. I think inside I knew I would have to choose a path at some point. Tough kid or good kid. It wasn't too long before that opportunity would come.

One of the other opportunities they offered us in school was to be assigned to the traffic boy squad. We controlled the traffic flow going by the school. I was a regular on the squad and made the rank of sergeant. As an extra reward for being traffic boys, we were given a free trip to Treasure Island.

Treasure Island was an artificial island in San Francisco Bay one-mile-long by 3/4-miles wide. It was built in 1936 for the 1939 Golden Gate International Exposition and subsequent World's Fair. With acres of thrill rides and shows, it was a kid's dream land, long before Disneyland. With Treasure Island as the carrot, and Principal Wilson's whippings as the stick, I stayed mostly on the straight and narrow in school.

By the early 1940s, shoeshine routes had given way to regular shoeshine stands. In this day of hustle, adults had set up shop in prime locations. One of the most successful men in the neighborhood was Mr. Bell. Rare for a Colored man at that time, he owned ten houses, three shoeshine stands, and two moving trucks. When I was 12 or 13, on weekends, my buddies, Pete Penn, Lonnie Boy and I shined shoes at one of his stands, and loaded and unloaded furniture from his moving trucks all day. Jobs had become very scarce, so the most we could command was fifty cents for a day's work.

All of us worked hard. You didn't slack, because your friends would have to pick up that slack. My family was counting on me to bring home my share. Fifty cents doesn't sound like much today, but back then it would buy five loaves of bread. Chances to double that daily salary didn't come around often. So when one such opportunity arose, I took it.

One day when we had finished working, Mr. Bell said, "Tell you what, boys. I'll race you from one telephone pole to the next. If you beat me, I'll give you a dollar for today's work, but if I win, I pay you nothing."

It was an easy decision. We worked ten hours to make 50 cents; we could run for a few seconds and double it. We would have been fools to turn it down. And this wasn't going to be work at all. It was play. The kind of play we did all the time. We simply had to run a race.

We were all pretty good athletes, except for Lonnie Boy. He was short and chubby, but boy could he play the piano. I never understood how short, chubby fingers could move so fast. He came from a family of musicians. You could hear it whenever his mom called him home for dinner, "Oh Lonnie Boooooy," she sang in beautiful echoes across the neighborhood. Lonnie Boy was no athlete, but even he could beat a forty-year-old man in a sprint.

The rest of us could trounce the other schools in football, basketball, and track on a regular basis. Baseball was a different story. Jackie Robinson hadn't broken the color line yet, so, despite the barnstormers, we had no one to idolize in baseball. It held no interest for us. We could catch, we could jump, and we could certainly run. We could definitely beat an old man in a race to the next telephone pole to double our salary for the day. I almost felt guilty. Almost. Mr. Bell could afford it, and I could already see my mom's face when I brought home that cash. Or maybe I would just keep it and buy myself a hamburger and a shake.

Me and my buddies grinned at each other as we all stood even with the first pole. The orange sun was still partially visible over rooftops in the distance. A cool west coast breeze at our backs.

I would have to be cautious at the start as the sandy grit that had settled on the cooling asphalt could steal my traction if I took off too fast. We knew this, of course, because we ran on these streets all the time. There was a slight pause between Mr. Bell calling us to our marks, and to get set, before he barked "GO."

As planned, my start was measured, cautious of my traction, and with the knowledge that I did not have to exert myself to beat the old man. Within four steps, I was at full stride. The stride that ran touchdowns and won hundred yard dashes. The stride the girls cheered for at football games. Easy pickin's.

In a sprint, you usually know halfway through where you stand. You know how much energy you are expending, you can hear the breathing of your competitors, and peripherally you can see where they are. You can feel their exertion.

At the halfway mark, I took note of where everyone was. Lonnie Boy was already way off the pace, Pete Penn and the other boys were slightly behind me, which was cool. But I wasn't racing them. I was racing to double my wages. Of course, I didn't need peripheral vision to know where Mr. Bell was. He was already well in front of me. And he was striding with ease.

The effort to increase speed in a sprint is counterintuitive. You want to push every muscle, every fiber in your body to work harder, but by doing so, you simply tense up, which slows you down. You actually have to relax. A thirteen-year-old boy, seeing a day's wages literally moving further and further out of reach, cannot relax. The vision of disappointment on my mother's face did not put me at ease. With each stride, I thought about the couches I had lifted, the boxes I had carried, the stairs I had climbed to earn that money. Five loafs of bread. I began thinking about how I would tell my mom that I had lost all the money I'd made that day. I was running in quicksand.

The smirk on Mr. Bell's face as he turned to watch the rest of us listlessly cross the finish line, told us what he had known all along; that he could beat us. This had been no gamble for him. This had been a way to sucker a bunch of naïve kids out of their wages. We had been hustled. He made no attempt to forgive the bet. The lesson I learned on the street that day is that there is no easy money in life. A lesson that I would need to draw from later.

4 ENFORCER

My junior high years were a time of coming in to my own. Like others my age, I explored, I tested boundaries. I was growing in to manhood. Junior high was when I experienced my first French kiss.

Carmella Stout's cousin was visiting from Texas. I had worked my way up to a kiss when suddenly she stuck her tongue in my mouth. I jumped back, startled, which just made her laugh. It wasn't the last time someone from the opposite sex would seek to teach me the ropes.

One thing I saw Dad do, time and time again, was to stand up for people that could not stand up for themselves. I wanted to emulate that. When I saw someone being treated unfairly, I stepped in. I enjoyed unmasking a bully or two for the cowards they really were. I ran with a rough group of guys. I took pride in being an enforcer, taking care of kids that couldn't fend for themselves.

One of the bullies was called Boo-Boo Lester. He was always looking to start a fight. One day, as I was walking behind him, he tempted fate by tossing a half-finished ice cream bar over his shoulder and down my shirt, trying to provoke me. It worked. The fight was short, with him on the losing end. It sent a message to the rest of the school that Boo-Boo Lester was all bluster. No one was afraid of him after that. I made sure of that. But one day, I would take the enforcer thing too far.

Admittedly, I grew up in an environment where breaking the law was part of the fabric of my life. I saw prostitution. I ran numbers. I saw shake-downs by the police. My father ran a gambling house, whose customers carried switchblades in their shoes.

But there were also many positive influences in my life, beginning with my father. The message that transcended all of the extracurricular activity was that he worked hard to provide for his family. There would be no begging, and certainly no empty stomachs. On occasion, the county government gave out shoes and blue jeans to the families of kids that needed them. Families like ours. And we received the monthly box of staples from the government – flour, sugar, salt, canned milk, jam – but nothing more. And there would be no stealing. No taking of what we hadn't earned. No cheating your fellow man.

Opportunities also opened up for me as I matriculated to Herbert Hoover Junior High School. I learned how to do mechanical drawing. I could draft, and draw buildings with perspective. I could create something from a blank sheet of paper. I also still had my knack for woodworking. It was there that I began to see possibilities beyond my neighborhood. It was there that I decided that I wanted to become an architect.

There were opportunities at home too. Uncle Spencer and my father would let people pawn almost anything so they could gamble. One day, my dad came by a couple saxophones: a soprano and later a C melody sax. He brought them home, I learned to play them, and got into the school band. Plus I was pretty fast, so I had a place on the track team. And then, of course, there was that kiss.

So there I was with my persona forming: athlete, architect, musician, lover, enforcer. These personalities were all at my disposal. I was all of those and yet not fully any of those. Sometimes they clashed and a dominant personality emerged.

One afternoon, my best friend, Raymond Gutierrez, and I were playing in an inter-class volleyball game at the junior high gym. It was being refereed by another classmate of ours, a kid named Ramee. I don't know why, but Ramee was doing everything he could to make sure the other team won. At least, that was what we thought. Every call he made was in their favor. And with every call, our team got angrier and angrier. Me and Raymond knew the rules, and so did Ramee. But he wasn't calling the game fairly. Needless to say, we lost the match. We were athletes, we hated to lose. More importantly, we were a couple of bad asses. We were still in school of course, but that didn't mean we couldn't have switchblades of our own.

When the match finished we followed Ramee outside around the back of the gym. As he turned the corner, we cornered him right where no one could see us. Yeah, he was scared. You could see it in his eyes. This just made us bolder, of course. The more frightened he became, the tougher we were. And there were two of us, and just one of him. We grilled him on why he was cheating. He had no answers, only denial. We were fully justified. He knew it just like we did. Raymond got in his face and slugged him in the arm. Hard. I already had extracted my small switchblade from my shoe. I cupped it and had it hidden behind my leg just like I had seen it done. Ramee never saw it coming.

I could feel the knife penetrate his skin as the knife passed through his trousers and into his left thigh. I had never used my knife before. It didn't feel like I thought it would – like it did when you saw it in the movies. In the movies there was no searing look of panic from the victim's eyes that traveled to your soul. There was no wash of nausea as the knife was retrieved, now red with the blood of another kid. There was no decision to be made about cleaning the knife before sticking it back in my shoe. No rush of adrenalin as we fled the scene, leaving him screaming with pain. No, there was no satisfaction of vengeance that I had been promised. This tough guy thing was a lie.

Instantly, I felt horrible. On the way home, I threw the knife in the sewer, not to try to hide the evidence – there was no hiding from what I had done – I just wanted to distance myself from that knife, and that feeling, as quickly as I could.

It didn't take long for us to get called in to the principal's office, along with my mom. I will never forget the look of disappointment on her face. That hurt more than any ass whuppin' the strap could ever deliver. We were expelled of course; which meant more time to sit around the house and see my mom's face. She had raised me to be better than that. I swore that when I got back to school, I would never make her that disappointed in me again. I didn't know at the time, but I wouldn't have much of a chance.

After serving a lengthy suspension, I was allowed back to school. I knew I had taken the enforcer thing too far, and I didn't relish trying to be the enforcer again. And I didn't until it was thrust upon me.

***

We left school one Friday for the weekend. That Friday was December 5, 1941. This meant December 7, was a Sunday. The Herbert Hoover Junior High we went back to on December 8 wasn't the same Herbert Hoover Junior High we had left the Friday before. We were shell shocked. Angry. We huddled in cliques and wondered aloud what was next. Being on the west coast, with no Pearl Harbor to defend us, we wondered if we were next. No one even knew exactly where Pearl Harbor was. We were scared, and we were anxious. But our feelings of anxiety were dwarfed by what the Japanese-American students had to be feeling. When they weren't being whispered about and stared at, they were being outright confronted, spit on, and attacked. The tension was palpable. I had known Harry and Henry Mizote since I was four years old. They were like brothers to me. We also hung out with Joe Morita, Take, Nobu and many other Japanese-Americans. They were just as shocked as everyone else. But they were also embarrassed and ashamed. They were Americans. It was all they knew; all they were. Unfortunately their ancestry connected them to the country that had attacked us. People didn't see them as Americans. They were viewed as the enemy. But my friends and I were a close knit group. There was no question that my loyalty was with them. I no longer carried a knife, but I was still an enforcer. And I hung out with a pretty tough group. The bullies knew that if they messed with our Japanese friends, they would have to deal with us. So our friends were left alone. At least until the US government pulled their trump card.

The corner grocery store was run by Mr. Sakamoto and his wife. It was a staple of the neighborhood and made a comfortable living for the Sakamoto's and their baby girl. The neighborhood was so closely knit that Mr. Sakamoto allowed people to purchase goods on debt. He maintained a ledger, and people paid when they could – usually every month or two.

The US started interning Japanese-Americans in February 1942, just three months after the bombing. It was just a matter of time before Harry, Henry, and my other Japanese-American friends would be taken away. Mr. Sakamoto and his family would not be spared either. One day, before impending internment, Dad had gone in to pay his bill when Mr. Sakamoto thanked him profusely, and told him that many people had stopped paying their bills after the bombing. Not only were people blaming Japanese-Americans for the war, but they were anticipating their internment and believed they could get away with not paying their debt. Mr. and Mrs. Sakamoto still had bills to pay, and they had a young child to take care of. They had to make what they could before they were interned. So Dad took Mr. Sakamoto by the arm along with his ledger and together they knocked on the doors of all of his customers, and "Big Walt" demanded that they pay Mr. Sakamoto what was owed. I think I know where I got the enforcement gene.

After internment, land laws in the west coast states barred all Japanese-Americans from owning their pre-war homes and businesses again. The Sakamoto's lost their home and business. Harry and Henry lost their home. And I never saw my friends again.

5 MOM

The 13th Amendment, abolishing slavery was ratified on December 6th, 1865. Thirty-six years later, on September 25, 1901, a young plantation laborer named Sarah gave birth to my mother, Jennie Williams. Jennie was just a child of twelve when she gave birth to her first son, my half-brother Herman. This was not by choice. It was difficult growing up in the early 1900s, even more difficult growing up as a Colored person on a plantation that still clung to the barbaric rules of slavery. There was no justice when a plantation owner decided to have his way with the daughter of one of his Colored laborers; even if she was still a twelve-year-old child. By the time she met Dad, my mom Jennie already had three children: Herman, a daughter Myrtle, and another son, Alges.

With such a stark beginning, the odds of a happy

life were not in her favor – unless she had the gumption to defy those odds.

Mom took on the world as it was. She was beautiful, with smooth dark skin. And although she never learned to read, she handled all of the finances, and was a wiz with money, and jigsaw puzzles. Dad, an amorous, engaging, industrious, family man had taken her away from swampy Louisiana to California, the land of promise. Two of her brothers also migrated to the California shipyards, so she had family there as well. Together, Mom and Dad would have five more children. Herman, her first son, lived to reach the age of ninety-four.

Mom was very social. She and her good friend Miss Penn loved to sip their wine and chat. Although at some point, the frequency of "sipping" seemed to increase. I didn't yet know why.

For fun, Mom and Aunt 'Stelle would put on their Sunday finest, which included the fine stockings with the seam running up the back, catch the C-Train for a nickel, head to the middle of the Bay to Yerba Buena Island, and then take the ferry to San Francisco. San Francisco was like the Emerald City to Oakland's Kansas. When Mom and Aunt 'Stelle stepped off of the ferry, they looked like they belonged. Sporting her favorite gold hoop earrings, set against her beautiful skin, she would leave the house looking like a movie star. They window shopped all afternoon, pretending they were deciding what to buy, when all they ever had in their purses were a couple sandwiches and some fruit.

Mom was the one that would lead the family to church every Sunday. I was always proud of the way she looked. She always had a smile and a hug for everyone. After church, each of the kids got fifteen cents – ten cents for the movie and five cents for snacks. The movies were a treat, but that fifteen cents weighed heavy in our pockets, and the thought of winning the fifteen cents in our buddies' pockets was too much to bear. So, more often than not, we ditched the movies and headed to Robertson's Rugworks to beg for one of the scraps of carpet that was laid out or hung in the drying yard, because a scrap of carpet made the best surface for rolling dice.

Scooter, who was a grown man, was always lurking around the corner to jump into our game when he saw us on our knees forming a small circle. Being older and wiser than us, he won all of our money time and again. If we did happen to win, we would be gone about the same time it took to watch a movie. But if we lost the money quickly, we would be home much sooner. When we came home too soon, our parents seemed upset. It didn't occur to me until I was much older that those Sunday afternoons were the only time they could be alone.

They weren't happy when we crashed the party.

Because Mom could not read or write, she dictated letters to me, and I wrote them to Herman while he was still living in Houma, Louisiana. Later, Herman and his wife Clara joined us in Oakland. Being so close in age, Mom and Herman grew up more as brother and sister than mother and son. When they were together, Mom would make a pot of coffee, and the two of them would sit in the kitchen and talk. While Herman stayed with us, he felt obligated to help out financially, so he paid rent. This didn't sit well with his wife, Clara. That probably contributed to Herman and Clara splitting up later.

Because Mom started cooking at such a young age, by the time she had a family of her own, she was quite the cook. Chitlins, red beans and rice, fried chicken, macaroni and cheese; they sound like standard fare, but she could take the monthly government staples and whip them into a scrumptious meal. And, of course, nothing went to waste. If you didn't finish your dinner from the night before, it became your breakfast in the morning.

I was the one designated to keep Mom stocked with wine. Mom enjoyed her Muscatel because it was sweet. You could buy wine at any age back then. Even as a young boy, she would send me to Mr. Sakamoto's to refill her bottle. I would greet

Mr. Sakamoto, head to the wine barrel, pop the cork on the bottle, turn the spigot on the barrel and fill the bottle. He would then note the debt in his ledger. Mom liked beer too, so Dad would bring home Bullseye beer from time to time. He could buy a whole case for $1.20.

At some point, the trips to Mr. Sakamoto's for wine seemed to increase. I loved my mother, but I was never comfortable seeing her slur her words and walk with a wobble. I never said anything to her, but it made me angry. Dad later had a hospital bed rolled in for her so she could sleep more comfortably. I never connected the long, low moans I heard at night to the need to numb the pain with alcohol. It wasn't until she died that I finally understood. By then it was too late for me to say I was sorry for my anger.

Dad knew it was coming, but it didn't mean he was ready. It was early afternoon when he got the call. I was with Dad, Uncle Spencer, and Grandma at the boarding house. We raced back to the house, breaking all traffic laws along the way. With tears streaming down his face, Dad pumped Mom's cancer laden chest and tried to breathe life into a body whose spirit had already left. It was 4:45 PM April 1, 1944. I was fifteen. Mom was forty-three.

6 HIGH SCHOOL

I attended Oakland Technical High School. Notable alumni include Clint Eastwood, Dave Brubeck, the famous jazz pianist, and John Brodie the former NFL quarterback. When I attended, World War II was in full swing, and patriotism dominated everything we saw, heard, or thought about. I had gotten pretty good at playing baritone and bass saxophone, and had joined the Reserve Officers' Training Corps band. Once a month, those in uniform, including those in the ROTC, were given free passes to the theater. We were very proud to wear our uniforms whenever we could.

One afternoon, me and two buddies, marched in perfect step, five or six miles, all the way downtown. It didn't matter that one was Jewish and the other Chinese. When we put that uniform on, we were all the same.

The technical high school was just that. It was designed to give kids who were not destined for college, a trade they could build a career around: automobile mechanic, welder, refrigeration repairman, electrician, woodworker, for example. I also ran the 440 and broad jumped for the track team. With all of the distractions I had, I still couldn't fill the hole left in my heart after losing my mom. Every day it was harder and harder to get out of bed. I lost interest in school. Went less and less, and eventually dropped out completely. Hey, my dad dropped out after 8th grade, and so did Uncle Spencer. My mom never even went to school. I would be just fine if I didn't go back.

It broke my father's heart. No one with our family name had ever finished high school. He was sure that I would be the first, but I was done. Dad couldn't, or wouldn't say anything because I was still contributing to the household income anyway I could. But one day, Aunt 'Stelle found him on his knees, crying.

Aunt 'Stelle and Uncle Spencer had divorced by this time, but Aunt 'Stelle was special to me, so we stayed very close; even closer after Mom died. I could confide in her about anything. And she knew how to motivate me. She had been working on getting me to go back to school. I think she knew I was close to going back on my own. I just needed one more push.

One day I visited her and she promised to make my favorite meal if I agreed to return to school the following semester. I agreed, and she rolled out Aunt 'Stelle's red beans and rice, and a lemon meringue pie. I ate until my stomach hurt, devouring all of the red beans and rice, and all of the pie – save one piece. Aunt 'Stelle seemed to also arrange to have a girl I was sweet on – Jean Robinson – stop by around the same time. I had to share a piece of pie with her.

When I did go back to school, I didn't want to return to Tech. I wanted a fresh start, so I went to University High School. Most of my friends from North Oakland went to school there. By all standards, it was a high performing school. Good teachers, coaches, one of the best choirs in the city, and top athletics. Among its notable alumni are 1936 Olympic 400 meters gold medalist Archie Williams and his classmate, tennis great, Don Budge. Plus, it was walking distance from my house.

I immediately connected with a group of guys to hang out with. There was even a mentor in the area they were anxious to introduce me to. She went by the name of Ms. Bush. They made it easy to meet her, and were even nice enough to walk me to her house. As we approached her house and passed a very large hedge, three or four of them grabbed me and threw me into the large hedge. I realized then that hedge was also a bush. "Meet Miss Bush!" they yelled, laughing as they ran away. Jokers!

We seemed to have more than our share of characters at university. One was Kermit Scott. Kermit was the king of nicknames. A young Black girl and a large White kid, both of whom had large backsides were named Big Tocks and Little Tocks. A Black girl with a large pompadour hairstyle was called Monster Ball.

We also had some of the best athletes in town, especially in the dashes and high jump. Our high jumpers were so good that when we competed with the schools on the east side of town, our guys would argue over who was going to come in first so they could get their name in the newspaper as that week's winner. Keep in mind that the other team was still jumping, but our guys knew that they could beat them by four or five inches.

I did better on the track team than I did in football; I ended up on the JV football team that first year. No matter, in one of our games I ran three touchdowns and threw a pass for another.

Some of our female teachers were students from the University of California, Berkeley. They were not much older than we were, so me and the guys were always trying to get their attention. University made it fun to go to school again.

Unfortunately, University High closed its doors for good at the conclusion of WWII. In September,

1946 I attended my third high school – Oakland High School, which was way on the other side of town. Life at Oakland High would be very different than what I had experienced so far.

The stares were something that I had not experienced before. Not like this. With each class I attended – English, math, history – my anxiety increased as I failed to glimpse even one Colored guy. I saw a couple girls, but no guys. Not in the parking lot, not in the classroom, not in the hallways, not in the bathroom. I was immersed in a sea of White faces. As the day continued, I looked more and more forward to football signups, where I knew the "brothers" would at last congregate.

I spent an entire day, going from venue to venue, engaging with hundreds of people, and not one of them looked like me. The gym offered more than refuge; it would make me feel normal again. Just feeling normal was an enormous relief. But my shock reached its peak when I entered the gym. Not a black face to be found. Not one. Oakland High had great athletes. They were just all White. The most famous was Jackie Jensen, who would be inducted into the College Football Hall of Fame and win a World Series with the Boston Red Sox. And Zoe Ann Olsen, Olympic diver, who later married Jackie.

I found out that there was only one other Black guy, Sam Shelton, and eight Black girls in all of

Oakland High. All of them came from North or West Oakland. There were only five or six Black families that lived in all of East Oakland. And not one east of Telegraph Avenue, as no homes were sold or rented to Coloreds there.

The only guys I recognized at football sign-up were a few White guys that had come over from University High School. Paul Jones was one of those guys, and he helped me survive. Other than that it was not a warm welcome. When I carried the ball, instead of trying to knock me down, the first tackler would just hold me and wait for his buddies to come and lay some licks on me. Even when I was on the ground guys would get hits in after the whistle. I was the fastest guy on the team, but I couldn't run forever. They were trying to get me to quit. But every day, at the end of classes, there I was strapping on my helmet. Ready for more.

After a few weeks, with the protection of my friends from Uni, and my refusal to quit, they got to know me and eased up. Ultimately, I became one of the stars of the football team. Helping the team win games was an elixir to acceptance, and ultimately I was at least tolerated, and by some, even liked. Later, I joined the student Block O club and was voted in as Sergeant at Arms.

After three high schools and a one-semester sabbatical, I became the first Jourdan to graduate from high school. The year was 1947. Even so, my father didn't attend the graduation. I know it was very important to him. Maybe he felt like he didn't belong, or that he would embarrass me. It did hurt. I never asked him why, and he never volunteered an explanation. I vowed that if I ever had children, I would never miss an important event in their lives. Of course, that promise would be tested.

7 COLLEGE

Work two hours - earn two meals. I worked two hours a day bussing tables in the cafeteria. That's what passed for a scholarship at City College of San Francisco in 1947. But I wasn't complaining. I was nineteen years old. I was playing football in college, going both ways: offense and defense. That's what everyone did in those days. We wore leather helmets and jerseys with thin padding underneath. It was a mentally and physically exhausting game. Even taking its toll on young men. I was always hungry. Always. My belly never seemed to be full.

The Dean of Men that got me the job in the campus kitchen also got one for my new friend Ray Urbano. Ray was a Philippine-American football player. The two hours we worked earned us breakfast and dinner. But our hours were from 11:00 AM to 1:00 PM. Lunchtime. And we weren't allowed to eat. An expectation that a nineteen-year-old athlete would not eat lunch was an unreasonable expectation. Luckily for us, the kitchen was run by hotel industry students. We quickly befriended them and enjoyed the fruits of these friendships by receiving sandwiches and big slices of cake. Ray and I would take turns sneaking the food into the bathroom, locking the door, and devouring the sandwiches in five or six huge bites. The cake, always moist and fresh, went down easy - chased with tap water from the faucet, we were quickly back to work.

The administration was all about making education affordable. City College was a model of affordability. All I had to do was purchase a student body card for $5.00, buy my own books, and pay lab fees. The Women Accepted for Voluntary Emergency Service (WAVES), had abandoned their barracks at the end of the war, and the barracks had been converted in to dorms. We paid $12.50 a month to stay in those converted barracks. That rent was eventually waived by another job the dean got for me, performing light labor tasks around campus. For spending cash, I joined the Navy reserves. In addition, me and two new buddies – one Jewish, and one Irish – sold coffee and donuts while everyone was studying. We also sold clothes that were seconds, telling people we had bought them out of the back of a supplier's trunk and that they were "hot."

San Francisco City College had been voted the 1946 football national champion for junior colleges the year before I arrived, so as a freshman in 1947, I was ecstatic to make the varsity. I had everything I wanted. I was going to college, studying architecture, and playing football on a nationally ranked program... if only I had remembered to go to class.

I was too busy hustling for money, chasing girls, and enjoying my time in the reserves to study. Despite the low probability that the US Navy would take Negro pilots, I had developed an interest in flying. The Navy reserve unit I joined operated out of the Oakland airport. Under the guidance of full time sailors, I learned to repair and maintain all sorts of aircraft; the F4-U Corsair, the AT-6 Ryan, and several torpedo bombers. In order to test our repairs, we were required to start the planes and run them through a series of checks with the engines up. This meant climbing in to the cockpit, strapping on the belts, starting them up, and dreaming of one day flying those beautiful machines. On occasion, the pilots would take us up on training runs, and we would sit in the navigation seat or torpedo seats. All of that was much more exciting than school. Biology, math, English held no interest for me. I didn't need those things to design buildings. I was good at that. I had earned A's in all of my drawing classes in high school, and I thought that was all I needed to become a successful architect. I learned the hard way that that was not how college, or life, worked. Once Coach Klemmer got word that I was skipping classes, I was demoted to junior varsity. It got my attention, and I had the whole year on JV to think about it.

Although I'd been demoted, I kept my job in the kitchen, and Ray Urbano and I developed a bond that lasted well into our sunset years. On a team full of Polish-American's, we referred to each other as Jourdanski, and Urbanski.

By the way, after Ray left college, he found his way into the entertaining world of professional wrestling and became well-known in the industry's fledgling years. He was one of the first to paint his face and create an alter-ego. Taking advantage of the lasting hatred of the Japanese, and his Asian looks, he took on the persona of Tokyo Tom. He'd gladly take a staged pummeling if the price was right. He lost a lot of matches, but he made a lot of money. We ended up living near each other in the 1970s, about 60 miles north of Los Angeles in Port Hueneme. In his early forties, Ray was diagnosed with a brain tumor. Fortunately, it was found to be benign. After surgery, he regained his health and got back in the ring. He wrestled for several more years and lived another thirty-six. Renaldo "Ray" Urbano passed away in 2002 at the age of seventy-eight.

In my second year at CCSF, I made it back onto the varsity. That was not a given, and there was no free pass. Several Negro students – yes, we were Negroes now – had tried out, but only seven of us made the squad: John Fortson, Rotea "Jughead" Gilford, Ollie Matson, Frank Puckett, Burl Toler, Edgar West, and me.

On offense, Jughead and I rotated at right halfback, and I backed up Ollie at left, so I had to know both positions. I started on defense at left corner opposite Jughead. Jughead and I were fast enough to play tight bump and run, running all the way downfield backwards. If anything got past us, which was rare, Ollie was there as safety to clean it up.

Ollie was truly a gifted athlete. After college, he earned a silver medal at the 1952 Olympics in Helsinki as the lead-off man for the US in the 4x400 relay, and he got a bronze in the 400. Later, he became one the best running backs in NFL history, playing for the Chicago Cardinals, Detroit Lions, Los Angeles Rams, and Philadelphia Eagles. He was an all-league selection from 1954 to 1957 and was voted MVP of the 1955 Pro Bowl. When he retired in 1966, after fourteen years in the NFL, he was second only to the legendary Jim Brown in combined rushing yardage. He was inducted into the Pro Football Hall of Fame in 1972, and College Football Hall of Fame in 1976. Ollie passed away on February 19, 2011 at the age of eighty-one.

My new friend Burl Toler was no slouch either. Burl hadn't played football in high school, so he joined the team as an unknown. Burl dwarfed most people. Broad shoulders and huge hands made him a natural. In the 1940s, it was common knowledge that Negroes were not allowed to play quarterback. But we were also not allowed to play center or linebacker. The linebacker position was considered to be the quarterback of the defense, and the Center was the leader of the offensive line. Negroes were not considered smart enough to play those positions. Burl Toler changed all that, at least at CCSF, by dominating both positions. In his first practice at linebacker, he stopped Ollie cold, four plays in a row. After the fourth stop, Ollie reached up his hand to introduce himself to Burl, and a bond was formed. Burl started at center AND linebacker. He was a 9th round draft pick for the Cleveland Browns, but suffered a career-ending knee injury during the college all-star game and never played a down in the NFL. Undeterred, he continued to be a trailblazer. He became the first Black NFL official, and in fact the first Black official of any major American sport. He was also the first Black secondary school principal in his school district, and the first Black official to officiate the Super Bowl. The world would lose Burl in August 2009 at the age of eighty-one.

Ultimately, all seven Negro football players from that 1947 team would go on to enjoy successful professional careers – quite a feat in the 1950s.

Rotea "Jughead" Gilford distinguished himself as a highly decorated San Francisco police officer and the department's first Black homicide inspector.

Edgar West enlisted in the marines after CCSF, and served five years of honorable service. He used the GI Bill to complete his degree in electrical engineering and later retire from Kaiser and the City of San Francisco after serving each for over twenty years.

John Fortson graduated from UCLA, and later taught business at SW Community College while enjoying a successful career in real estate.

Frank Puckett entered military service in 1954. He too was honorably discharged, and was bitten by the entrepreneurial bug, owning and operating his own electronics repair shop in San Francisco for several decades.

And then there was me.

I didn't know it at the opening of the season, but the 1948 CCSF Rams were on a path to make history. With Ollie leading on offense and Burl on defense, teams began to dread when we came to town. Everyone, that is, except Modesto Junior College. Modesto was led by their running back Otris Williams. Otris had been named All-City in four sports at nearby Oakland McClymonds High

School – the same High school Bill Russell attended. He was 5' 11", and weighed 210 lbs. That was huge for a running back in those days. Everyone knew Oltris, and he did not take kindly to the likes of Ollie and Burl stealing the headlines.

We came into the game against them that year undefeated, and Oltris was looking to change that. To put it lightly, he was a handful. Usually, the first man to make contact would either bounce off, or hold on until one or two other teammates came along to help drag Oltris to the ground. He gave us all we could handle, but we hung on to beat them by a touchdown, which was the closest anyone came to beating us all year. We finished the year 12-0. Our dominating defense allowed only 62 points all season – an average of just over five points per game. And for the second time in three years, CCFS was voted the junior college national champions.

After football season, I got a job cleaning a restaurant across the street from the school. I was eating more, and exercising less. My weight quickly skyrocketed from a football-playing weight of 175 lbs., to a restaurant-cleaning weight of 200 lbs. I started going to the gym to work off the weight, and that's when I got into boxing. Combative sports – boxing and martial arts – are the most mentally and physically demanding for one simple reason: you rest, you get hit. Usually hard. I couldn't take any time off between the bell. I had to learn to keep moving. And to do that, I had to be in tip top shape: and that meant both cardiovascular-wise and with muscle development. After a few months learning to box – and stay alive – I got my weight down to 172lbs. The light-heavyweight division. It was a leaner, more muscular 172 than I had been before. I was like a rock. I sparred as a light heavyweight.

Our number one heavyweight at the gym, Tufele Suega, was a Samoan who could hit like a mule. One day, I came in for my workout and learned that Tufele was in need of a sparring partner. None of the other heavyweights had shown up. My guess is that they were looking for a day off from taking a beating. So coach grabbed the next best thing: me. I was a running back first and a boxer second, so I relied on my fundamentals as a runner and kept as much distance as I could from Tufele, while coming in often enough to get my shots in. Well, I didn't die, which also meant that I passed my audition, and the coach asked me to join the team.

I had won my first nine matches when I entered the ring against a guy who had a lot more experience than me. I wasn't afraid of him, but my coach had opted to attend an NAACP meeting that day, and that meant I had no one in my corner to help me with strategy against a tough opponent. I ended up losing my only match of the year that day. Beaten on points. It left an impression on me about the importance of coaching.

The Negro players from the football team hung out at Ollie's house on Divisadero Street quite often during the off-season. His mom always served up something good to eat along with guidance for getting through school and staying out of trouble with young girls. Burl and I had girlfriends, and both of them lived on Sutter Street. We visited them at night and invariably stayed there later than we should have. The challenge was finding a way back to the dorms. The good news was that a taxi was $1.35, no matter where you wanted to go in the city. The bad news was that City College was about as far away from Sutter Street as could be. If we told the taxi driver we were going to City College, he would just speed away. So we would say we were going to Fillmore, which was nearby, and then hop in the cab. Once we were rolling, one of us would say, "Hey, it's still early, let's go see what's happening at City College," and the driver had no choice but to take us there. It was like running an option play.

Although I stayed at the dorm, I went back home regularly for some home cooking. Dad had remarried in 1947 to Menomonee Truehill Pierce. Menomonee had two sons, Howell (Dutchie) and John (John-John). From Dad and Menomonee's union came Menomonee (Toni), Joyce Brenda (Brenda), Spencer, and David. Together with me, Robert, Delores (Laurie), and Jimmie there were ten kids. Nine of the ten of us finished high school, and the tenth, Jimmy, received his GED while in the Air Force. That was a rare accomplishment in those days.

On one trip back home, I took a couple of college friends to the Sunset Club, a bar in our neighborhood. We were enjoying a beer when someone called out to us. I looked up to see that it was one of the working girls I used to run errands for, Long Goodie. She was leaning against the bar, talking to a couple of the men. She looked the same: caramel-colored skin, high cheekbones and round inquisitive eyes. Not much older than me, she worked at the brothel near my father's house.

"Hey, you," she yelled, looking over at the three of us. We looked at each other, not clear who she was calling out to. "You, in the middle." She nodded her chin upward, gesturing at me. "Come here." My buddies poked me with their elbows, showing me knowing-grins. I feigned surprise, pointing to myself and responding, "Me?"

"Come down here." It was more of a request than a command, but delivered in a way that I couldn't decline. I made my way over somehow, without removing my eyes from my shoes.

"Aren't you Little Walt?" she asked with an easy smile.

I managed a smile in response.

"Look at you, all grown. What are you doing

these days?"

"I'm going to college now," I responded proudly. It was the rare young man that made it to college those days. Between war and hard times, college was considered a luxury that many could not afford. It was indeed a rare exception for a young negro.

"I'm playing football and studying to become an architect."

"College! Well, you are doin' very well for yourself."

I managed to move my eyes to somewhere between my shoes and her face, catching everything else along the way. I could feel my buddies' eyes drilling into the back of my head. I was going to hear about this later. I had to be cool.

"How have you been, Miss Long Goodie?"

"Quite well actually," she said. "In fact I just bought myself a new car. It's right out back, want to see it?"

I knew my friends couldn't hear the conversation, but I still felt the need to turn back and look at them. Seeking advice. All I saw were huge grins and nods of approval. It didn't matter that they couldn't hear.

She wasn't really waiting for an answer. "C'mon," came the command/request as she tapped out her cigarette, and grabbed her purse.

I followed her outside as she proudly showed me

her new car. I was unable to hide the surprise on my face.

"I know what you're thinking," she said. "You all think we are just a bunch of dumb working girls beholden to Miss Nessie. Well, we do the exact same thing our customers do, but we get paid for it, so I guess we aren't so dumb after all," she said this with a smile. I smiled too.

"Most of us are better at business than the men we spend time with. I even have my own duplex. I live in one unit and rent out the other. That's my retirement plan for when I get too old to work."

More exposed surprise on my face.

"C'mon, I'll show you."

Directing me to the passenger's seat, she hopped behind the wheel. Handling the manual transmission like she was born to drive, she took us to her place, which was in a very nice part of town. Her neighbors probably had no idea what she did for a living. I'm not really sure she would have cared.

"You like beer?" she asked.

"Sure," I said. I doubt many people said "no" to Long Goodie.

"Come on in and have a beer. I'll show you my place." Her place was well furnished, and comfortable. The beer was cold. She directed me to sit on the couch.

I finished my first beer while telling her about

college, and football, and boxing. Into my second beer, and clearly relaxed, she shifted the discussion.

"I bet those college girls are all after you, aren't they?"

My eyes found the tops of my shoes again.

"I do all right." This was the truth. I wasn't shy, and I had been with my share of girls. But Long Goodie added perspective.

Looking me dead in the eye she challenged, "I bet you have no idea how to take care of a woman, do you?"

Whatever I mumbled in response she quickly dismissed with a flick of her hand.

"Here," she said, reaching over to relieve me of my half-consumed second bottle of beer.

"Why don't you go and take a shower," she commanded/requested.

"Why do I need to take a shower?" wanting to retract the words a soon as I said them.

"You just go take a shower, and then let Long Goodie teach you how to properly take care of a woman."

Off to the shower I went.

* * *

After the summer of boxing I rededicated myself to studying and earned my associates degree at City College. The following year, Jughead and I transferred to San Francisco State. We were veteran college football players, with a national championship in our pocket. We were anxious to show them what we could do. But to Jughead's consternation, his past would catch up with him.

He had dropped out of high school in 1945. They didn't catch it at CCSF, but they did at State. State would deem him to be ineligible. That left Marv Crews, Rudy Smith, Mel "Good Foot" Haynes and me as the only Negros to make the team. Marv and Rudy were left and right halfbacks. I was the fullback, and Haynes did a good job at end. Our quarterback was an Italian-American called Sam DeVito. Our coach, Joe Verducci, also Italian-American, decided to dub us the "All Dago" backfield.

Without Ollie in the backfield, I got a lot more carries. During the homecoming game against Chico State, I ran a pitch out about sixty yards, and got bumped out inside the ten. After doing the yeoman's work to get us that far, I was sure I would get the call on the next play to take it in the end zone. Instead, the coach called a play for Rudy, and he scored the touchdown. This didn't sit well with me, so the next time we got the ball to the twenty, and they called my number, I told Marv not to get in my way, 'cause I was going in, and I did.

The following Monday, I was hanging out near the gym between classes when someone grabbed me saying, "We've been looking all over for you, where've you been?"

"In class," I said. Apparently, no one had bothered to look there. The guy pulled me into the auditorium, which was full of people who all cheered when I came in. The San Francisco Chronicle had voted me outstanding player of the game.

We went on to win the Far Western Championship that year and we traveled to Medford, Oregon to play Lewis and Clark College in a bowl game. This was my first introduction to corn-fed farm boys. They were big, and they hit hard. So hard that I committed the first and second fumbles I had had all season. Our second string fullback fumbled too. Needless to say, we got our butts kicked that day. It was a long bus ride back to Oakland. What was ironic, and unbeknownst to me, was that I had made my future wife very happy that day. She was a cheerleader for Lewis and Clark.

The winter after football season, I had contracted pneumonia and was laid up in the hospital for five days. All that time alone gave me an opportunity to reflect on my life, and where I was going. I wasn't applying myself in school, and I had lost interest in architecture. The Korean War was in full swing. The draft board was knocking at the door, and I knew I didn't want to be drafted by the Army. I decided to take things into my own hands.

8 NAVY

On July 26, 1948, the summer before my CCSF Rams were crowned national champions, President Harry Truman signed Executive Order 9981, desegregating the military. But almost two years later, at 0400 hours on the morning of June 25, 1950, when North Korean troops stormed across the 38th parallel, the United States military was still not fully desegregated. The units that were partially desegregated only assigned Negroes to servant roles, like mess stewards and transportation specialists. I had an opportunity to be one of the new recruits to change that.

My hope was that I could be a draftsman, but all of the drafting for the navy was contracted out to civilians in Port Hueneme, California. So that was not available to me. I came out of boot camp with some of the highest scores they had seen, and I had experience as an aviation machinist from my time in the reserves. I was a shoe-in to become an aviation machinist in the navy. So when the San Diego assignment officer recommended that I become an aviation machinist, I could not have been happier.

The only problem was that the aviation machinist school was in Pensacola, Florida. Pensacola sounds like a great place to be, unless you are black and it's 1951. Jim Crow laws were still in full effect. Negroes were second-class citizens, required to sit in the back of the bus. It would be four more years before Rosa Parks would challenge those laws, and another fourteen years before the Voting Rights Act would be signed, clearing the last obstacles for Negro voters. Living in the south meant that I would be drinking from segregated water fountains, using side doors to buildings, barred from restaurants, and sitting in the back of buses. I was a proud, Black man, and I never shied away from a fight. If I relocated to Florida, it would not end well for me.

So I looked the assignment officer in the eye. "I'm not going to Pensacola to be treated like a second-class citizen," I said.

"You're in the navy, son, you'll do as you are told," he retorted.

"There are only two things I have to do, sir: be Black and die." With that I spun on my heels and left his office.

When I returned from boot camp leave to learn of my assignment, I was surprised to learn that the assignment officer had obliged my demand to not be sent to Pensacola. It reinforced my instincts to stand up for myself. That felt good. That good feeling would not last long.

Unfortunately for me, the navy was about following orders, not individual preferences. To impress on me the way things worked in the navy, the assignment officer had assigned me as a deckhand on an LST: Landing Ship, Tank. This was to be a horrible assignment for several reasons. An LST is notoriously slow. With a top speed of 8 knots, it would be a monotonously slow trip from San Diego to the war zone in Korea. But more disconcerting is its purpose. LST is just what the title infers. Tanks are loaded onto the deck and it carries the tanks and the tanks' crew right up to the beachhead. LSTs played a prominent role in the landing on Normandy beach in WWII. They were nicknamed Large Slow Targets by their crewmen. Being a deckhand on an LST was not what I had in mind. I would essentially be cheap labor. I was going to be used to load tanks on and off of the ship while under fire. Not exactly a taxing mental exercise. This is not something I wanted to be a part of, but the assignment officer had made clear to me who was in charge.

The Korean War was in full swing, I wasn't any more afraid of combat than the next man, but I at least wanted to have a fighting chance. Nonetheless, I was assigned to the OGU (Outgoing Unit) as a deck hand on an LST, preparing for deployment to Korea. I had to think of a way to improve my situation.

The Navy Training Center (NTC), SUBPAC, AIRPAC, and the Marine Training Base at El Toro, were like four-year colleges on base. To boost morale, and to ensure regular athletic activity, the navy had instituted football competitions among these groups. It was like playing in a small college or a junior college league on the base. Coaches were always angling to stock their teams with good talent.

While awaiting our deployment, I was assigned to a grass cutting detail. During a break, I made my way over to the NTC, and introduced myself to the athletic director/football coach. I was still in great shape. With my background, and a national championship on my resume, he immediately saw the value of having me on his team. Just two hours after introducing myself to him, he had pulled the right strings to have me withdrawn from the Outgoing Unit and assigned to him at the Navy Training Center. I would not become cannon fodder for the North Koreans on an LST.

Coach knew I was a starting cornerback at

CCSF, but that I had backed up Ollie at halfback on offense. Because I started on defense at CCSF, and not on offense, he assumed I wasn't as good on offense. So he never gave me a chance to run the ball. As a result, he and I never developed any chemistry. We had a falling out, and I was soon transferred to the Sonar school.

I was quickly installed in the sonar group's offense. Most of the football programs had kids that were just out of high school. I had already played college ball and, at twenty-two, I was bigger, stronger, and faster than most of them. As a result, I ran two or three touchdowns every game. The coach at NTC happened to be scouting a game where I piled up a bunch of yards and ran two touchdowns. After the game, he mentioned to a colleague that he didn't know I could run the ball like that. I said, "He never gave me a chance." In an odd bit of synchronicity, I later learned that the NTC coach also coached Hugh McElhenny, a future NFL star who was related to the Tabasco McIlhenny's that had owned the planation my great-grandfather was from. Six degrees of separation.

As fun as football was, that wasn't why I was in the navy. The sonar assignment officer had seen my test scores and asked me how good my hearing was.

"My hearing?" I asked.

"Yes, this is the sonar group: sound navigation and ranging – sonar. Your tech scores are good. If your hearing is good, I can make you a sonar technician." My hearing was great!

The sonar techs were the eyes and ears for the destroyer escorts or DEs. Two technicians worked in tandem. We generated a sound – a "ping" – and transmitted it through the water. An object in the water caused an echo to return. We used the time the echo took to return to estimate the distance to a potential target. We would classify the object as a sub, a non-sub – which usually meant a mine – or undetermined. If a target was detected, a DE could attack with "hedgehogs" (a type of mortar launcher) and depth charges, or signal for more firepower from the fleet. A tech could only work for 20 or 30 minutes at a time. Longer than that, tone deafness would set in, and the ping may not be detected, or the distance may be miscalculated. Operating in open water was a deadly game of hide and seek. We feared subs the most because they could attack from great distance, but mines could do serious damage as well.

I was excited about the prospect of using my brain to be a vital part of the crew. Upon graduation from sonar school, I was assigned to the 7th Fleet. The 7th Fleet, which patrolled the Pacific, commanded some 60 to 70 ships consisting of battleships, aircraft carriers, destroyers, and a myriad of supply and support vessels. I was assigned to a DE.

I learned quickly that I had a knack for Morse code too. Something all sonar techs were supposed to know, but not all of them did. Sonar techs were expected to be experts.

Sailors were always sharing a beer at the Enlisted Man's Club. So I knew the technicians in the class behind me and ahead of me. Two friends from the class ahead of me were assigned to the USS Ernest G. Small. The USS Small was a gearing class destroyer. At almost 400 feet long and 40 feet wide, it carried an arsenal of six 5-inch guns, twelve 40 mm anti-aircraft guns, eleven 20 mm anti-aircraft guns, depth charges, and torpedoes. But none of that mattered if the sonar tech didn't detect a target.

It was October 7, 1951, and the USS Small was providing screening service for an aircraft carrier in the war zone. On larger ships, like the USS Small, the sonar shack was located under the chow hall, which was below the water line. The sonar shack was a quiet spot where the technicians congregated when they weren't on duty, which is what nine of them were doing when the two who were on duty failed to detect the mine. The resulting explosion blew a hole in the bow so large that it was completely severed from the rest of the ship. All nine sonar techs residing in the shack were either killed. Eighteen other sailors were also injured. Miraculously, the captain was able to save the ship and have it towed back to Pearl Harbor for repairs.

The incident served as reinforcement to those of us preparing to ship out about the importance of our roles. An undetected threat put the entire crew at risk.

I was assigned to the USS Wiseman. The Wiseman was a Buckley-class destroyer escort. Smaller than the USS Small, the Buckley-class was only 306 feet long and 36 feet wide. It was home to fifteen officers and nearly 200 crewmen. Because it was smaller, the sonar shack was located forward of the open bridge, above the water line. It was a relief to learn that. However, to take readings at the end of our shift, we were required to venture below the water line. Each time I did, I thought of my friends who had died on the USS Small.

Our mission was to screen in protection of elements of the 7th Fleet on the east coast of Korea. We would be part of a screening force set up by several other destroyer escorts (DE). We carried out patrol assignments, and provided anti-submarine and escort services for replenishment groups.

To provide these protection services, the Wiseman partnered with three other DEs: the DE-441 USS Seiverling, the DE-442 USS Moore, and the DE-449 USS Hanna. Each DE was capable of screening an area 2000 yards wide. The four DEs lined up in parallel, overlapping areas of responsibility by 500 yards. By working together, we could cover a range roughly 6,500 yards wide in front of the fleet. We needed to maintain this alignment because submarines would look for gaps in our spacing, creating an opportunity for them to slip through and wreak havoc in the rear of the convoy. If they were successful in slipping past our coverage and explosions started, we couldn't hear and sonar would be useless. Because we were in the front of the fleet, we were always at the greatest risk.

Once we left port and steamed towards the war zone in late 1952, the excitement of screening for a huge battle fleet gave way to boredom. Steaming through miles and miles of endless sea, day after day, became monotonous.

One evening, after reaching the war zone, we intercepted a small boat off the coast of North Korea. It was manned by four men and a young girl. They said they were trying to escape from North Korea. They had clearly been on the water for several days. They were disheveled and weak, and they emitted the second-worst odor I would smell on this assignment. But we could not take them at their word. The North Koreans had not taken care of their people and the captain was concerned that despite their appearance, they were part of the North Korean Navy, and they had been laying mines. The North Korean's did not have much of a navy to speak of. They operated only forty-five small vessels, so we could not assume that this small boat was not on a more covert mission. Once we had them on board, cleaned and fed. We turned them over to the South Koreans at Yang-do Island. Before leaving the area, we attempted to shell and sink their vessel. I say "attempt" because it was too small to hit. After several failed attempts, the frustrated captain called in an air strike and blew the ship out of the water. We cheered.

We had not yet encountered the North Koreans at sea, but we did have a close encounter with their allies, the Russians.

I had become one of the best sonar men on the ship. I had a good ear for recognizing patterns, and I was one of only two of the eight sonar techs that could read and send Morse code. One day, while on duty, I heard what sounded like a submarine. North Koreans had no subs, so it had to have been a Russian sub. The Russians were technically not in the war, but being a fellow communist nation, they did what they could to assist. The Russian subs, we knew, followed the fleet as we steamed towards the combat zone and reported our numbers, our content, and our location to the North Koreans.

Not only did I recognize the distinctive "ping" of a submarine coming from our starboard quarter, but I also heard cavitation; the sound of her engines churning. I reported my finding to the second class sonar tech in charge. Upon identifying an enemy sub, our action would be to "roll two"; roll over to where she was, and roll a couple depth charges over the fan tail. The Russians would not initiate engagement, but they would defend themselves if attacked. Wary of this, the second classman refused to classify it as a submarine. He classified it as undetermined – meaning no action would be taken. Better not to wake a sleeping giant, he thought. We continued on without disturbing her, but I will swear till my grave that the sub was lurking there.

On other days we attacked North Korean supply lines. One day, for seven hours we tracked a North Korean train moving along the coast, looking for the right time and place to engage. Unable to hit a target moving that fast, the captain again called in air support. The planes hit their mark, sending the box cars into violent cartwheels.

On many occasions we had to encourage the enemy to engage in order to divulge their position so we could call in airstrikes from the Canadian Air Force. We had such a mission one evening in early December of 1952. It was a typical subfreezing night in Inchon Bay – a clear enough night for us to be spotted, should the North Koreans seek to engage. Our mission was to venture into mine infested waters in enemy territory, close enough to the 155 mm North Korean artillery batteries hidden on the mountainside, to be spotted by a North Korean forward observer. If we could entice them to fire on us, we could reveal their location. Taking out the battery would allow our ground troops to move closer to their objective. In a perfect world, the 155 mm battery would fire at us, miss, and we would quickly vacate the area before they could bracket us and fire for effect. In an imperfect world, they would hit us. These were the risks of war.

Late in the war, the Hanna, one of our sister DEs took a hit in the aft fireroom from North Korean shore batteries, killing Sailor Robert Potts. Potts was the last shipboard casualty killed by enemy action during the Korean War.

Our mission that day, therefore, was to draw fire without getting hit. I had finished my 1200 to 1600 hours watch, and prepared to rest up before returning to my sonar-post again at midnight. It was 1900 hours, or 7:00 PM. I had just nestled into my pillow, sinking into that level of sleep only achievable on a porch hammock or a ship being slowly rocked by calm seas. Abruptly, I felt the Wiseman take a hard shudder. I sat up, unsure of what to make of it. A few seconds later I felt it again, and then again. "GONG, GONG, GONG!" The signal for battle stations sounded over the loud speaker!

Sailors slept ready to roll most of the time, in a state of half-dress to respond quickly if called to duty. Heart pounding, I leaped out of bed and only had to put my shoes on before sprinting towards the ladder.

On any combat vessel, the crew is trained to react to a call to battle stations. You don't want 200 men making up their own minds about what to do, where to go, and how to get there. We are trained, with simple straightforward instructions. When battle stations are called, all 198 enlisted and 15 officers have a place to be. It is one of the few times that the entire crew is all moving at the same time. To facilitate that movement, we had been instructed to move along the starboard side of the ship (right side) if you are moving towards the bow (front), and to move along the port side (left side) of the ship to move aft (back). Effectively, everyone was to move about the ship in a counter-clockwise fashion. Knowing it would take me longer to reach my battle station if I stayed below and traveled through the superstructure, I made my way to the ladder that would take me directly to the outside. Flying up the ladder, I emerged through the hatch to find people scampering in every direction. Counter-clockwise rotation be damned. There was no order, no discipline, and no explanation as to what had happened.

It was like running through a thick defense in the middle of the pitch black night, bouncing off linebackers. My duty station was the range recorder. My job was to determine the distance to the nearest threat. This is what we had trained for. The ship was counting on me to do my job without error.

Breathless, I reached my battle station at the range recorder and made my way to my seat to access the sonar panel. It was dark outside. I was to be the eyes and ears of the ship. I asked the lead tech, "What do we have on the scope?"

He looked at me like I had spoken a foreign language. "We don't have a scope," he said.

I responded with an open mouth and no words. There had been no explosion, so we had not been hit by a torpedo, and we had not hit a mine. But we weren't moving. We were well within range of the powerful North Korean 155 mm guns, and we weren't moving. "What?" I asked with a mixture of fear and incomprehension.

The lead tech banged on the panel and flipped the switches. The screen stared back with darkness. All of a sudden sailors raced in from the bow, traveling at the speed of fear, along with the answer. One reported between breaths, "We ran aground and sheared off the sonar dome." And then he said the four words every sailor fears, "We're taking on water."

It didn't make any sense, we were at least two klicks (kilometers) from shore, and we had a draft of 13.5 feet. The bottom of the ocean HAS to be deeper than that.

"How could we have run aground?!" Before I had finished the question, I knew the answer.

The Bay of Inchon was notorious for wide swings in tide level. The tide change at Inchon can be as much as 31 feet in a single day. The US fleet learned this the hard way at the beginning of the Korean War. Ships needed to heed this warning and be keenly aware of water depths, even several thousand meters off-shore. Sand bars sound innocuous, but can render a ship helpless if you run up on one. We had run aground. We were completely immobile. We were blind, and we were taking on water. We were suddenly at the mercy of the North Korean artillery that, a few minutes before, we had been enticing into firing at us. Now we were praying that they did not see us at all.

Sailors manning our gun batteries had seen the sand bars approaching, but their warnings to the officer of the deck had gone unheeded.

The second warning that had been disregarded was from the sonar technician manning the depth finder. The officer of the deck had ignored him too. After the grounding, the sonar tech anticipated that he would be accused of not warning the officer of the deck, so he pulled the charts and hid them for safekeeping to cover his ass – proof that he had recorded and reported the risk.

Sightless, stranded, sitting in the target area, taking on water. I sat at my battle station completely helpless, waiting for an artillery shell to land. We were far away from help, as we were there as lone bait. Be careful what you ask for.

Teams scrambled to try to contain the freezing sea water that gushed into the gaping holes. Hammering, welding, yelling, praying. We murmured our fears to team mates who sat close by. The ship continued to shudder as we took on more seawater. If only there was something I could do, I thought. I could only sit and wait. One of my shipmates, an otherwise tough talking Texan was unable to control his bowels, and suddenly soiled himself. He didn't have to tell us; everyone knows the smell of human feces.

We spoke in hushed tones for no apparent reason. The pounding and yelling from the work crew was enough to give our position away to a sub or land-based listening post. We remained at battle stations. Our gun crews stood ready to return fire, if fired upon.

The crews hammered and welded as we waited for the moon to do its work and call the tide back to shore. Minutes, then hours, passed. We needed the tide to come in so we could leave, but if the tide returned before the breach was repaired, we would sink. Finally, after the longest three hours of my life, the USS Wiseman began to slowly rock. The first sign that the tide was returning. The crews had done their job and sealed the bow. The pumps sent the sea water back where it belonged and the ship began to rise. We cautiously backed off the sandbar, turned around and slowly limped home for repairs.

* * *

Over thirty-six thousand US soldiers and sailors lost their lives in the Korean War, but the USS Wiseman and her crew emerged from the combat zone with no casualties. After surviving the scare in Inchon Bay, the Wiseman steamed back to Sasebo, Japan, for initial repairs, and then to Yokosuka for major repairs. When leaving dry dock at Yokosuka, the captain managed to hit the submarine net, ripping the sonar dome off once again. That was one sonar dome too many, and he was relieved of duty.

This did not detract from the fine job her crew did in providing screening action for the 7th Fleet and its missions in the Pacific. We were a proud crew, and we were ready for some serious R&R in Hawaii. My buddy "Whiskey" Wilkerson and I shared a beer in the galley before hitting the town. Our target was a little bar on Hotel Street – the notoriously fun destination for soldiers and sailors on leave. We had visited a particular bar there on our way out to Korea. There was one chocolate-skinned beauty that sang in one of the bars. For several days we had talked about seeing her again on the way back. We wanted nothing more than to share a couple drinks, forget about our time in the war zone, and hear her sing. We had been shot at, and lost some buddies from the Hannah when she was hit. There is no feeling like surviving a close encounter to make you appreciate life. And no prouder feeling than having served your country with honor, and feeling respected for it. There was a lot of patriotism that ran through WWII and continued into the Korean War. Decked out in our white uniforms, we floated down the street on a cloud of pride and honor.

We found the little bar we had visited on the way out. It was an inviting site. We were smiling as we approached the door. There was a large but friendly looking Samoan bouncer to greet us.

"How you doin', man?" we inquired.

"You fella' look like you had too much to drink," came his witty reply. Witty because we'd only had one beer each, so we knew he was joking. We laughed as we gave him a knowing smile and stepped towards the door.

He slid in front of us and repeated his statement, "You fella' look like you had too much to drink." He wasn't smiling, and neither were we. Then it dawned on me. "You don't want us to come in here do you?" I asked.

After WWII, soldiers returned home looking for jobs. But the south had not industrialized and there was an acute lack of employment there. As a result, many southerners stayed in the military. So many, in fact, that they dominated the ranks. The military, particularly the army, took on a distinctive southern bent. Most of the senior enlisted ranks – the senior non-commissioned officers – came from the south, and brought with them their southern view of segregation and treatment of Blacks. They had also positioned themselves to take ownership of key entertainment establishments in and around army and navy bases – particularly in Hawaii. They owned the bars, and they hired the bouncers.

As big as this bouncer was, he caused me no concern. I was 180 lbs. of solid rock. I was a boxer. I had just come from the war zone representing these United States, and I was being denied entrance, again, because of the color of my skin. I was pissed. And I was going to show this bouncer exactly who I was.

Suddenly, there was a hand on my shoulder. But it wasn't the bouncer, it was Whiskey talking me down. "It's not worth it, Walt. Come on, don't get yourself in trouble. Let's just go somewhere else."

I looked at the big Samoan and could see the sadness in his eyes. He was just following orders. He didn't want to do it. He had probably been treated unfairly himself. Taking it out on him would have done nothing to change our circumstances. We turned and walked away.

I had been discriminated against all of my life. This was nothing new, but this time it dug deep. We had served our country. We had earned the right to be treated as men. It took just a few minutes on American soil to be reminded that we were Black. I told myself that I would never return to Hawaii again.

9 RUBY

The three White men dragged the Black woman for several blocks. Her knees, smeared in dark crimson, buckled from exhaustion. Her screams had the opposite effect for which they were intended. Instead of them being tools of appeal for her release, they served to strengthen the men's resolve and amplify their satisfaction. Her face was a blend of torment and tears.

Asa Leland Brock had heard that the Ku Klux Klan operated like this, but he had never witnessed it before. The spectacle was being played out in broad daylight. The men were brazen. They were bold. They were untouchable.

Word on the street was that they were dragging the woman off to question her about the whereabouts of her husband. She had refused to tell them what they wanted to know. The husband had committed some unknown affront to the Klan, and they wanted to bring him in for justice. Klan justice, because in Mississippi in 1917, the Ku Klux Klan *was* the law.

Asa was 16, and he was not alone watching this travesty. There was a crowd; White and Black. But Asa felt alone. It was as though he was the only one who was outraged; the only one who was disgusted; the only one that was scared. He was filled with dread about his life, and his future. He would not live like this. He would not stay in Mississippi.

Asa had relatives in St. Louis. He didn't know much about St. Louis, but he knew it wasn't Mississippi. He would hitchhike, jump the train, whatever he had to do to get there. Without telling his parents, he left home.

Once he arrived in St. Louis, he searched for his relatives. He found them, and they promptly sent him back home to Mississippi. Undeterred, Asa ran away again, back to St. Louis. This time he would never return to Mississippi. He joined the Union Pacific railroad as a waiter, working the route from Chicago to Portland, Oregon.

Letitia Patterson had an exotic combination of African and Caribbean roots. Her mother had passed away when she was 13, so her father who had emigrated from the Caribbean Islands, raised his two daughters and two sons himself. Mr. Patterson had mastered the five tiered organ at the

Baptist Church of St. Louis – without the ability to read music. And he made sure the children were in church every Sunday. That's where Letitia met Asa.

Asa would see Letitia in church when he had Sunday's off. They fell in love, married, and started a family. Asa's train route took him to Portland several times each month, and he grew to love the northwest. So, despite there being a law in Oregon prohibiting Blacks from living in the state, he convinced Letitia to raise their family there. If ever they could afford a home, they would have to find a White friend to purchase it for them and transfer the title to them surreptitiously. Letitia was a school teacher in St. Louis, but because of her color, she wasn't allowed to work in Portland. So she stayed in their rented home to raise their four beautiful girls, each two years apart: Rose Marie, Ruby, Joy, and Beverly. They were the only Colored children in their classes all the way through high school. The nicknames of choice from their classmates were "Nigger," "Darkie," and "Pickaninny." Joy joked that she didn't know her real name until she was in the 5th grade. Although with each Brock girl the school seemed to slowly become more and more accustomed to the young Negroes, they were never fully accepted. Of the four, Ruby seemed to emerge as the most feisty, the one less willing to accept their lot in life. One day, when Joy was twelve, she complained to Ruby that there was one girl in particular that bullied her relentlessly. Ruby insisted that Joy point her out on the way home the next day.

Ruby stealthily hung a block behind Joy as she walked home. The plan was for Joy to point the girl out when she saw her.

Halfway home, Joy spotted the girl across the street and motioned to Ruby who the bully was. Like a panther, Ruby darted across the street, grabbed the girl's arms, and held them behind her.

Years from then, when Ruby reached adulthood, she would top out at four feet eleven inches tall. She was always short for her age, but she made up for it with grit and determination. Her height would not stand in her way.

As Ruby held the girls arms, she called for Joy to cross the street, and ordered her to slap the girl. Joy, not one for violence, delivered a half-hearted slap to the girls face. This was unacceptable to Ruby, who ordered her to "hit her like you mean it".

Slowly, years of verbal and physical abuse from her classmates percolated to the top of Joy's consciousness. Years of being taunted, isolated, and teased came to a head. The girl became the focal point for all the abuse she had suffered year after year. Joy reared back and slapped her as hard as she could. Then she did it again, and again, and again.

Finally, Ruby released her, and the girl ran off in

tears - never to bother Joy again. Ruby looked at Joy, mouth agape. "I told you to hit her, not kill her!"

Despite the daily bullying and isolation, the girls excelled at school. Letitia couldn't teach in the school system, but she could teach at home. Asa had never finished high school, but early on, he and Letitia had agreed that not only would their girls finish high school, but they would go to college. As each reached the age of ten, the girls joined their sisters in the strawberry fields in the summer, picking strawberries to earn money, which they would save for college.

While Asa worked steadily as a lounge attendant for Union Pacific, Letitia squirrelled away money for college and to support their dream of owning a house someday. Asa typically shared a ride home with a friend after work. On one such day, Asa's friend told him he needed to make a stop at another friend's house before taking him home. When they arrived at the "friend's" house, the door flew open and Letitia came bounding out with a huge smile. She had saved enough money for a down payment on a house and bought it without Asa even knowing it.

Eventually, many neighbors warmed to the Brocks. The Brock girls were excluded from skiing and other activities available to Whites, so they became very creative at making up games in the neighborhood. As a result, the Brock house became the house all the kids gravitated to, to play games.

After high school, Rose Marie graduated from Lewis and Clark College, Joy from Linfield College, and Beverly from Monmouth College. Ruby became the first Black cheerleader at Lewis and Clark, and by doing so, Lewis and Clark had the first integrated cheerleading squad on the west coast. Ruby graduated with honors, and took a position teaching math in Oakland, California.

I would eventually meet Ruby in Oakland, but it was at Lewis and Clark that we first crossed paths. Well, sort of. She was a cheerleader for Lewis and Clark when my San Francisco State College football team traveled north to meet them in a bowl game. The second time we crossed paths, we actually got to meet.

I was stationed at San Diego, attending the high powered mine detection sonar school, and was on leave for a few days. I didn't expect much from the blind date that evening. I was really just going as Ollie Matson's wing man. My "play sister," Gloria, was sweet on Ollie, and asked me to help set her up. She promised me a date with a cute girl named Ruby Brock, a school teacher from Portland, Oregon. I walked into Gloria's family room, and Ruby took my breath away. She was beautiful.

We had a whirlwind romance. Every chance I got, I purchased an airline ticket for $14.95 from

San Diego to Oakland to see Ruby. I bought the engagement ring in the ship store of a mine destroyer, one of the actual ships used in the film the Cain Mutiny.

Six months after meeting, we decided to get married.

* * *

December 27, 1953. Two days after Christmas, and everyone was still in a festive mood. I took another long pull from the half pint of bourbon before handing it back to Earl. I was drinking to steady my nerves. Earl was drinking to make sure that I didn't drink the whole bottle myself. Having eloped with Ruby's older sister, Rose Marie, earlier that year, Earl was about to become my brother-in-law.

Behind the altar, behind the curtains, Earl and I sat alone on the hardwood benches in the back of the church. Dressed as best man and groom respectively, we passed the bourbon back and forth. Two days prior, my first choice for best man, Rotea "Jughead" Gilford, had informed me that he couldn't make it to the wedding. He just couldn't pull the finances together to make the trip from Oakland to Portland. So Earl had graciously agreed to step in. (Earl would become the first African-American to attain the rank of sergeant in Portland's police force.)

I had only made a couple of previous trips to Portland before the wedding, but as soon as I met Earl, he felt like a brother to me – which was especially good because no one from my family was making the trip to Portland either. No best man, and no family. Earl had my back.

This was to be a double wedding, the first double wedding that most people had ever attended. The youngest Brock daughter, Beverly, had already begun to plan her wedding when Ruby suggested that we make it a double. The other groom was Bill Hilliard. Bill had graduated from Pacific University, and was working his way up the food chain after starting as a copy boy at *The Oregonian*. He was on his way to become sports clerk, sports reporter, religion and general assignment reporter. Later, he would become *The Oregonian's* first Black editor.

This was also the first time many had attended a wedding where the guests were both Black and White. Asa and Letitia had fought through extreme racism and prejudice from the day they had arrived in Portland, and the community respected them for it. The Brocks neighbors had seen the girls grow up and were an important part of their lives. It was said that people put off dying to see who the Brock girls would marry. Beverly and Ruby were the last two.

The Brocks were as high society as Black families could be in 1950s Portland. Joy, the third

Brock daughter, was already married to Clarence Pruitt, a young dentist. And the reception for our double wedding would be held at the lavish residence of Dr. DeNorval Unthank, a prominent Black medical doctor and civil rights leader.

I peered through the curtain again. They were shoulder to shoulder in the pews. "Stop looking," Earl appealed. "There will only be more people every time you check."

I took another pull on the flask. It was empty. I held the bottle up high, trying to coax out one last drop. I looked out to the sea of faces. Hundreds of them, and I didn't know a soul. Alone, in a church of three hundred people. I had never been so scared in my life.

* * *

Bill and I made our way to the altar with our best men at our sides, waiting for the brides to arrive. All eyes were on us, in our matching tuxedos. We did look good. As soon as the organ played the first chord for *Here Comes the Bride* I could feel the tension leave my body. All heads turned to the back of the church, where we were already looking. Matching visions of beauty appeared. The pride in Asa's eyes was evident as he escorted his two daughters to the front of the church. He had married off all four daughters in the same year – to an honorable stable of gentlemen. He was a long way from Mississippi.

Dr. Unthank's house was equally packed. I fielded questions about my upbringing, my football escapades, and my time in the war. Everyone was warm and friendly. There were two separate rooms for the presents: one for us and one for the Hilliards. We took some with us, fitting as much as we could into Ruby's 1951 Crown Victoria. The rest would be shipped later.

We stayed as long as we had to before leaving. Ruby had planned our escape, and our destination. She had booked a beautiful hotel just outside the city limits. Wasting no time, we hustled to the room to do what newlyweds do. I was carrying the luggage, and by the time I had put it down in the room, Ruby was already half undressed. Carrying the luggage gave me an opportunity to scan the room. It was the nicest room I had ever seen.

"Wait," I said. "How much is this room?"

"Thirty dollars," she said, frozen in a state of half-dress.

"Quick, PUT YOUR CLOTHES BACK ON! We can't afford a room like this!"

I had been transferred from San Diego to Long Beach to Bremerton in the navy, and my paychecks had not caught up with me yet. We were operating on fumes.

We sprinted down to the front desk, told them

we couldn't stay, and then searched for a cheap no-tell motel. By the time we got settled, Ruby had developed a headache and there was no wedding night loving to be had.

We couldn't afford a honeymoon, so I settled Ruby in to our apartment on Ashby Street in Berkeley, and reported to Bremerton, Washington where I would commute for three months to work on the newly commissioned USS Jacamar, a converted Landing Ship, Infantry (LSI). Then I was transferred to the naval base on Treasure Island, the same island I had played on as a kid.

My responsibilities required me to be away several days at a time, and to stay on base. I sometimes had to serve on over-deck security watch, during which time I had access to a .45 caliber pistol. It would come in handy soon.

Ruby was a looker. A former cheerleader and sorority queen, she was always turning heads – whether she wanted to or not. One day I came home from work and she shared something with me that had been bothering her. One of our neighbors, an older married man, had been making lewd comments to her whenever he saw her walking up the stairs to our apartment. It didn't just bother her, it scared her. He knew I was away for several days at a time, and she was afraid he would try to take advantage of the situation. I had arranged to get home one day earlier than usual, at a time before

Ruby came home from work. I stopped by the man's apartment and asked him to come by my place to help me with something. I'm sure he was anxious to see the inside of the apartment so he could canvas it.

"Come on in," I said. He stepped inside and I said, "Hang on a minute." I went over to the desk and, without him seeing it, pulled the .45 out. I saddled back over to him and quickly pressed the gun against his temple. I had his full attention.

"Ruby told me about the things you've been saying to her."

If he tried to speak, he was clearly too scared to complete the task.

"If you so much as say hello to her again, I will blow your head off. You won't even look in her direction again. Do you understand me?"

He was breathing hard now. And nodding. Vigorously.

"Now get the hell out of here."

I didn't trust myself, and I didn't know how he would react, so I had field stripped the pistol and removed the firing pin. I couldn't have shot him if I'd wanted too. I could have just taught him a lesson physically, but this way he couldn't say that I had sucker punched him. The message was delivered and received. I never told Ruby, she would have been upset. But he never bothered her again. If he saw her coming in his direction, he would just turn around and go the other way.

* * *

I completed my obligation to the navy on March 15, 1955. It was time for me to pursue my first love, playing football. My old college friend, Ollie Matson, had been in the NFL for quite some time, and he was doing well. I had another friend that I had worked with on Treasure Island who had gone on to work for the San Francisco 49ers as a statistician. He had arranged for me to have a tryout. I headed home, excited to share the news with Ruby. The conversation was short.

"Honey, I've scored a tryout with the 49ers," I announced.

"You need to take your BA back to school and get your BA," she commanded.

There was no room to negotiate. The NFL would have paid me about $6,500 per year, which was great money, but careers were short. So I went back to school to pursue a degree in electrical engineering, and took a job as a driver with the Quick Way special delivery company at night.

The owner of Quick Way was a Chinese-American, who doubled as a driver. The other driver was White and, of course, there was me. We delivered packages all over San Francisco, so there was always someplace one of us was not welcome.

To accommodate for those racial limitations, the owner would shift the crew between the three of us, depending on where the deliveries would take us for the day. After lugging boxes for the better part of six hours, I would make my way to the highway and prepare to hitchhike home.

I never really knew when I would get home. It was a function of traffic, which direction they were going when they entered the highway, and the willingness of a driver to pick up a black man at 9:30 at night. I would walk to the highway entrance and pray that the car entering the highway at the intersection would be going my way. If it was, and if they were willing to take me, I would get a ten mile ride to Emeryville, and then walk about a mile and half, usually getting home around 11:00 PM. If I couldn't get a ride, I would walk three miles to a different route where there was more traffic, and then hitch a ride to find my way home. I would study as long as my eyelids would allow before falling into bed only to repeat the cycle five days a week.

Venturing into civilian life, we were still in the apartment on Ashby. So we found a nice neighborhood with homes large enough that some people had converted their garages into apartments, which they rented out for additional income. We rented a converted garage apartment in a predominantly White neighborhood. It was clean, freshly painted, and plenty of room for the two of us. We made it our home, and not long after we moved in, Ruby became pregnant.

We liked our home, but we found that, on those rare occasions when it did rain, water would seep in. It wasn't a healthy environment for Ruby, so we moved to a two-bedroom apartment. The apartment was set up over a store-front on Grove Street, across the street from the Catholic church. I would soon add father to the titles of student and delivery man.

Ruby stood 4 feet 11 inches tall, and was 90 lbs. on a good day. When she got pregnant, she resembled a snake that had swallowed a baseball. Skinny girl, big lump, more skinny girl. Going from sitting to standing was a lesson in balance and leverage. By the eighth month she was all waddle. The morning of March 11, 1956, she announced that it was time to go.

I packed her in the car, and delivered her into the hands of the good nurses at Berkeley Memorial Hospital. I was instructed on how to put on my gloves and gown and, once Ruby was prepared, I was ushered in to the delivery room. Ruby was a trooper, delivering our first baby boy. It was when he finally emerged and I held a complete, breathing, kicking, crying little boy, that it hit me that I was a father. That I had a child who was dependent on me.

I noticed a large lump on the side of his head. Seeing the concern on my face, the nurse assured me that it was a normal result of using the forceps to extract him and the lump would go away. She was right, and Walter David Jourdan, Jr. was indeed a healthy baby boy. We nicknamed him Skip.

When I finally left for the night, I secured a large bottle of bourbon, which I won in a bet with Burl's sister on the gender of the baby. I shared it with my father and my brother, Bobby, but I drank half of the bottle myself, and not even that could quell my excitement. The realization that I was a father, that I had a small human that looked to me for guidance and love, was enough to ensure my sobriety.

A new baby helped me strengthen my resolve to finish school. I had moved over to UPS to load and unload trucks for them, but I was only taking home $39 per week. On weekends, I worked in the back room of a local jewelry store.

Ruby made a little more than I did with her teaching salary, and that kept us afloat. I wanted to quit school at least once every couple of months. She would sit me down and talk me in to staying. "Stay the course," she said. She was my rock. We talked about having a larger family, but we decided to wait until I had graduated and had a solid job. My second son had other plans.

Fourteen months after Skip was born, along came son number two - born May 25, 1957. He was the recipient of the middle names from both of our fathers: Asa Leland, and Walter Thomas. We named him Leland Thomas. When Skip tried to say brother, it came out "Bubby." So they were Skippy and Bubby. Two babies, full time job, full time school, full time father. Sleep was the rarest of commodities.

After Bubby was born, we moved to a larger place on 54th street. It was a duplex in a predominantly White neighborhood. With Ruby's experience growing up with White neighbors in Portland, and my assimilation in the navy, we thought we would be OK. Much to our chagrin, everyone avoided us except one really nice couple across the street. The husband gave me a ride across the bridge to San Francisco every morning to go to school. The wife was always friendly to Ruby. She would often come by and have coffee or a glass of wine with Ruby. Word of our friendship reached the landlord of the house that they were renting, and the couple was ultimately forced to leave. With them gone, we were like a pariah in our neighborhood.

In July 1958, I graduated from Heald with a B average and a Bachelor of Science degree in electrical engineering. My life was about to change drastically.

One of my regular delivery customers was Bethlehem Steel. I had developed a relationship with a manager there. He learned that I was studying for my electrical engineering degree, and he already had a job lined up for me when I graduated. Ruby sent me out the door in my suit and tie for the interview.

The interview was short, and friendly. He already knew of my strong work ethic, and now I had a degree to leverage that work ethic in to a professional career.

"We've got a job for you," the hiring manager said. I was beaming. "We're going to start you off as an electrical technician and see where we go from there."

The air left the room. An electrical technician is barely more than a handyman. You simply had to understand basic wiring. It required no Bachelor degree; not even an Associate's degree. He could have hired me for this job a year ago. I'm sure he meant well, but it was difficult to convince people to hire Black professionals. Electrical technician just wasn't going to work for me. My disappointment was evident on my face.

"I'm sorry, but I didn't earn this degree to work as an electrical technician", I declined. I could answer any question they had, I could design circuit boards, but I couldn't change the color of my skin.

I returned home and delivered the solemn news to Ruby. She continued to support and encourage me as I secured an interview at Hughes Aviation. "We can do this!" she said to pump me up. I had set up an interview through a friend, expecting to be treated like a professional with a degree. Again, I was offered a job as a technician.

I couldn't believe that I had worked that hard, for that long, only to be treated like I was less than what I was. I had hit rock bottom. I knew I was technically strong. I had shown it in the sonar school. I had shown it learning Morse code. I had strong grades from Heald. All I needed was a chance.

Ruby had a friend at North American Aviation who she contacted to get me an interview. North American was the preeminent manufacturer of combat aircraft for the United States Air Force.

My interviewer, a White man, listened politely as I answered all of his questions, but he sat there with the same non-committal look that all recruiters gave me. When the interview concluded, he said, "Excuse me for a moment," and left.

My $39 per week was steady, but I wasn't bringing home what my family needed. I had a wife, and two kids the eldest of which had just turned two. I began to wonder if I should take a technician job if he offered one to me. I could show them what I was capable of, and then work my way up.

The interviewer returned, sat down and said. "I'd like to offer you a position as a design engineer. We can pay you $500 per month."

If he had looked hard enough, he would have seen my heart pounding underneath my shirt. I got to a phone as fast as could and called Ruby.

"Baby, I did it! I'm going to be a design engineer with North American Aviation. I'm going to be making $500 per month." That was about all I said. It was all I had to say. Then we just cried, and cried.

10 VOCATION

Moving in and out of your home was always an adventure, especially in our neighborhood. It took several friends, at least one of whom needed to be in possession of a pick-up truck. It took numerous trips, and many days, to complete the task. No one used a professional moving company. So when the massive *Bekins Moving and Storage Company* truck lumbered down the street, people started peeping out their windows. When the airbrakes hissed to a stop directly in front of our duplex, and the men hopped out and knocked on our door, the neighbors opened their doors for a better look. When the movers began carefully carrying our cherished furniture from our house and loading it on to the trunk, our neighbors had abandoned all pretense of not caring and stood outside staring, mouths agape, at what was transpiring before their eyes.

Ruby stood out front like a general directing her troops. "Careful with that. Yes, that will go in the living room. I hope that isn't too heavy." She knew the question was coming from the neighbors, and she had the answer loaded and ready to launch. Unable to bear it any longer, the nosey woman who hadn't bothered to say "hello" for the past two years, made her way across the street.

"You're moving?" she asked. It wasn't the moving that bothered her; it was that we were able to hire people to do it for us.

"Yes, Walt has a new job." Wait, let that linger, the hook is set. Savor the anticipation until she nearly begs for the answer.

"Really? Where?"

Ah, there it is - time to drop the hammer. Only then did Ruby turn to face her, better to take in her whole reaction. Better to test her ability to swallow her jealousy. "Walt has been hired as a design engineer with North American Aviation." She let that hang in the air for a moment, before adding, "He'll be designing circuit boards for their new weapons systems. You know who North American is, don't you?"

Everyone knew who North American was. They had built tens of thousands of aircraft that helped win World War II, and continued their legendary service manufacturing jets that shot down enemy MiGs in the Korean War. The neighbors were typically too stunned to even say "congratulations." But that didn't stop Ruby from reveling in every moment. Even when they stopped asking because word had spread, Ruby stayed outside to smile at the drivers that slowed to try to discern why a Bekins truck was in that neighborhood. And what they were doing loading the belongings of a Black family. Ruby was almost disappointed when the loading was done. Of course neither of us knew that the job at North American would not last.

We moved to a two-bedroom place in a nicer neighborhood on 65th St. between Harvard and Denker. A few months after I started working for North American, Ruby was having lunch with a girlfriend who worked there. The woman was an analyst whose job it was to reduce data from wind tunnel tests and supply the data to the engineers. Women with math acumen were being hired in to the aeronautics industry to serve as what were referred to as "human computers". Ruby had majored in education, but had a minor in math. She quickly determined that she had the aptitude to work as a wind tunnel analyst as well. She secured an interview, and within a few months of my employment, she was hired at North American too. We both worked on the acclaimed X-15.

The North American X-15 was a hypersonic rocket-powered aircraft operated by the United States Air Force and NASA as part of the X-plane series of experimental aircraft. It was designed to reach the edge of outer space and return with valuable data used in aircraft and spacecraft design. It set speed and altitude records in the 1960s, including the official world record for the highest speed ever recorded by a manned, powered aircraft It would continue to hold this record a half-century after it was developed. Ruby and I were proud to be on the team that made that aircraft a reality.

North American was in competition with other manufacturers to build fighter planes for the Air Force. In 1959, North American lost out on a substantial contract to one of their competitors, Republic Aircraft. Then, on September 23, 1959, North American suffered the cancellation of the XF-108 contract. Massive layoffs ensued, with Ruby losing her job in November of 1959, and me losing my job a month later. But now, not only did I have experience on the design team of some legendary aircraft, Ruby and I had made enough money between mid-1958, and the end of 1959 to become completely debt free. We were still renting at the time, but we had tucked enough money away to make a down payment on our first home. That was timely, because in March the following year, Ruby was pregnant again.

The layoff did not come as a big surprise. We could see the work dwindling, and everyone knew about the XF-108 contract cancellation. I was laid off on a Thursday. The next day, I made my way over to Packard Bell. I had heard that they were hiring engineers. While in the lunch room, I noticed a lot of people wearing Litton badges. Litton was involved in a venture with Packard Bell, and happened to have a number of employees in the Packard Bell lunch room. I inquired about Litton, and was told that they were hiring on 3rd St. in Beverly Hills.

I met with the manufacturing manager at Litton, Mike Vervich. He was impressed with my resume, and committed to calling me over the weekend with a firm offer. I had not been out of work for 24 hours and was about to be working again.

Unfortunately for Litton, when he called my house, Ruby answered the phone instead of me.

"Hello, I'm the hiring manager from Litton," he offered. "I'm looking for Walt Jourdan."

"This is his wife, Ruby, he's not home now, I will be happy to relay the offer to him," she probed.

"We are offering him a position as a design engineer with a salary of $500 per month."

"Well, North American paid him that right out of college. He's an experienced design engineer now. You'll have to do better than that." Ruby could be intense. By the time she had finished with him, I was making $700 per month.

After I started, I befriended the head of the computer department, who happened to be Black. I told him about the work that Ruby had done at North American, and soon she was working at Litton as well, as a computer programmer.

We purchased our first home at 1731 South Stanley Avenue in Los Angeles. It was a one-story, two-bedroom stucco home. The home cost $22,000 and came with a mortgage of $130 a month. We somehow managed to give the entire house a fresh new coat of paint without killing each other – which was no easy task. We installed a bunk bed for the boys, which became a triple bunk bed when our third son was big enough to use a regular bed. Brian Anthony was born on October 22, 1960.

At Litton, I was part of the team building the LN3 guidance systems for the F104 Star Fighter. Simply put, we built systems that kept planes on course, accounting for a phenomenon known as the Coriolis Effect which occurs due to the rotation of the earth. I became an expert at constructing the circuitry that managed the relevant on-board equipment. As the technology improved, new circuits needed to be designed. We designed the circuitry, and then our salesmen would sell the components.

Salesmen have a certain skill set. They need to understand how to convey the benefits of our products to potential customers, which means that they have to understand the features and functionality of our products. How did they work? Why were they better? Every few months, fresh batches of salesmen were brought in and it was my job to teach them the technical aspects of Litton componentry. Without the salesmen, we could not sell our components, without our engineers we had nothing to sell. What was obvious, to me anyway, was that I was both. I had been selling since I was nine years old. First shoeshines and then myself as I worked my way from one job to another. I knew I could sell. I was the combination that Litton needed to get someone with real knowledge in front of the customers. So I started attending classes at UCLA in the evening towards a graduate degree in marketing. I knew what I wanted to do.

But every time I inquired about a sales position, they were full. Only to have a fresh recruit sitting at my desk a few weeks later so that I could teach him the basics, about pitch and roll, and the Coriolis Effect. They never told me why they wouldn't allow me to move to a sales position. But I knew why. Litton wasn't ready to have a Black face as the face of the company. They needed to keep me in the back room, like the back of the bus. Different vehicle, same result. After four years and eight months at Litton, I was ready to leave.

I used my network to land a job as a manufacturing project manager with Interstate

Electronics in Anaheim. I had a strong team of engineers and technicians reporting to me. During the time I was with Interstate, we developed fifty systems that were used to operate the submarine-launched Polaris missiles. It wasn't sales, but I felt more appreciated there.

One day, about two years in with Interstate, I was having lunch with a friend of mine from Honeywell Aerospace. Known for its domestic products today, Honeywell is one of the nation's largest manufacturers of aircraft engines and avionics. It played a major role in equipping bombers for WWII, and participated in America's first successful earth satellite launches. They were also one of the first to get in to computing, competing with IBM in the early 60's. Half way through lunch, my friend popped the question. "So, Walt. Have you ever thought about sales?"

I almost jumped across the table. But I had to be as cool as I could. "Yes. For a long time now." I said. "But no one would give me a chance"

"We've been looking for a person of color to become a salesman for the last six months. We have guys that are technically proficient, but they don't have the marketing skills. And we have guys the can market, but the technical stuff goes over their head. I think you have both."

He invited me over to take a technical test, which I passed with no problem. That night they took me out for dinner and drinks. There was substantial drinking involved, but I was so hyped about the opportunity, the alcohol had absolutely no effect on me. The next day, they called and offered me a job. Once hired, my friend confided in me that they had decided the night we went out that, since they couldn't get me drunk, they might as well hire me. Welcome to Honeywell.

I became the first Black sales person at Honeywell. All eyes were on me to see if I would fail. I'm sure there were some who hoped I would, but they did not prevail. Most were very helpful, and very encouraging. There were those who had put their credibility on the line. I wasn't' there as a token, I had to deliver. Sales is an exposing profession. Either you sell or you don't. There is no in-between. After three or four months, they were impressed enough with my work that they asked me if I had any friends of color that had a marketing/technical skillset mix. I called my friend Bernie Hayes at Litton. Bernie was running a headhunting firm on the side that specialized in African-American professionals. He located a young USC student who Honeywell got on the payroll. The new guy absolutely tore up the track! After that, they just threw the door wide open. I had broken the color barrier at a major US firm. No one called me the Jackie Robinson of Honeywell, but I couldn't be happier with the way things worked out.

11 BROKEN

After five years in Los Angeles, Ruby and I could see the direction the city was going - and we didn't like it. One Sunday, while I was still working at Interstate, we piled the boys in to the station wagon and went for a drive. We stumbled into a sleepy suburb, which was closer to Anaheim than LA, called Rowland Heights. There was plenty of new construction. We signed a contract on a 2,356 square foot home for $28,450. It was exciting to drive out every couple weeks and see our dream house take shape.

When we moved to Rowland Heights, there were only five Blacks living in the city – and they were all in our family.

We didn't know it when we built our home, but as time went on and we ventured out, we noticed it more and more. But it wasn't all White either. Our next door neighbors were Hispanic-American's and across the street was a Japanese-American couple.

There was a healthy smattering of Hispanics in our town, and many more in neighboring towns. We joined the local Cub Scout troop and the boys flourished at school. The neighborhood was loaded with kids of the same age, and the boys did not want for companionship. There was just one family around the corner that wouldn't allow their boys to play with ours, but it was to their detriment, not ours. We never saw any overt racism the entire time we lived in Rowland Heights. There were subtle difficulties, of course. For example; as popular as the boys were, when they got older, their proposals to take their classmates to the Junior- Senior prom were always denied by wary parents.

Those matters were certainly not front and center when we arrived in Rowland Heights. At the ages of six, nine, and ten, the boys were all about playing with their buddies. We installed a pool in the backyard, and our house quickly became one of the "go-to" homes in the neighborhood. It was a beautiful two-story, four-bedroom home. Skip was already old enough to play Pee Wee Pop Warner football. I signed on as assistant coach, focusing on running backs and defensive secondary – the positions I played in college. The following year, Bubby – who now went by "Leland", was old enough to play, and my boys started at right and left halfback. They established friendships that they would enjoy for the rest of their lives.

We were living the American dream; unfortunately we were living it in the real world. The Great Depression was clearly the worst economic crisis in American history. The second worst occurred in the 1970s. The costly Viet Nam War was coming to an end. The oil embargo caused an extreme energy shortage, and the US was entering a period of high inflation and unemployment. Military-support industries took the brunt of the pain, and aerospace was no exception. Layoffs were rampant. Honeywell was not spared. In addition to the impact from the economy, the company received a lot of negative publicity for its involvement in the Viet Nam War and for its investments in South Africa, which was still practicing apartheid. As a result, Honeywell launched efforts to streamline their businesses and cut out less productive assets. New layoffs were announced almost weekly.

The axe was hanging over all our heads. We didn't know who would be laid off next. The anxiety was palpable. It created stress at work, and it created stress at home – eventually taking a toll on our marriage. Ruby and I started to have problems, and by the time I was laid off from Honeywell, Ruby and I decided to separate as well.

I moved out of the house with no fanfare. There was no tearful goodbye to the boys, I just showed up less and less until I didn't live there anymore.

But I promised myself that I wouldn't miss the important events. I would make every effort to show up at sporting events, graduations, and birthdays. When Brian was old enough to play football, I signed on as assistant coach. I wasn't going to do any less for him than I did for Skip and Leland. There was no way I was going to be absent from their lives.

I moved in with a friend who had a spare room in LA. It was in an area that was called The Jungle off of Martin Luther King Blvd., just west of Crenshaw. I looked for work wherever I could. No one was hiring. There was a flood of engineers in the market, and no place to go. After knocking on doors, calling everyone I knew, calling in old favors, I hit the bottom. There was no job to be found anywhere in the industry.

I had been a salesman for five years with Honeywell, so I leveraged my sales skills to land a job with Singer-Freidman, a manufacturer of billing systems that assisted doctors with their accounting. The job wasn't nearly as prestigious as being a technical salesman for Honeywell. But if I had to move down a rung to pay the bills, I did not hesitate. I applied the same work ethic that had always garnered success, and applied shoeshine-boy charm to close deals. By the end of the first year, I was the number one salesman in the country, winning a first class trip to Florida. So imagine my shock when the entire sales force was laid off the following year. The economy had continued to tank. Singer-Freidman decided to hunker down without growing, so the sales department was cut. Again, I was out of a job.

My success at Singer-Freidman taught me that I could sell anything. I sold watches wholesale for a watch manufacturer, and sold window security bars for a security company, but nothing stuck. Between 1971 and 1973 I had worked for four different companies. I was forty-four years old and had nothing. The friend I was rooming with in The Jungle had job issues too, and decided to relocate back to the east coast. I still had alimony and child support to pay, not because the law required it, but because it was my responsibility. I wasn't going to be one of those fathers that didn't take care of his family, no matter how little I made. Whenever I got a paycheck, no matter the size, I would break off a piece for Ruby and the boys. Divorced or not, I couldn't face them if I didn't. Ruby was playing the role of both parents at home. Managing three boys and their escapades on a daily basis was not easy. Being a single, African-American mother, some thought she would be an easy target to get the better of. They didn't know Ruby Jourdan.

One day when Lee was in grade school, he and one of his friends, Bobby Harrison, were playing in the large, open, dirt lot just up the street from our house. The lot was actually two lots, roughly a half mile square each, both rectangular in shape, upon which a future elementary school would be constructed. Built on a hill, the first lot was at an elevation of twenty or thirty feet above the second lot, which sat ten or twenty feet above a row of newly constructed homes. The kids referred to it as "School Hill", and would often go up there to play baseball, or just run around. Because the neighborhood was still under construction, these empty lots became an unfenced storage site for construction equipment, and a haven for young adventurous boys - much like the trains we played on when I was a boy.

One such piece of equipment was a cable spool. It resembled a spool of thread, but the ends, or "wheels" were five or six feet in diameter, and held thick wire cable. On this day, when Lee and Bobby ventured to this natural playground, the spools were empty, begging to be played with.

They were heavy. Built from solid wood, and bolted together. It took both boys leaning into one of them to get it rolling. How cool, they thought, to push it down the slope from the upper lot, to the lower lot. And so they did.

Once it reached the slope between the lots and rolled down, it picked up speed and hit the lower lot with momentum. So much so that it continued across the lower lot, and headed for the next slope that led to the new homes.

The boy's smiles slowly evaporated as the heavy spool rolled closer and closer to the far side of the lot – with plenty of speed. Those smiles then morphed into fear as the spool rolled over the edge, down the next slope in to the backyard, and through the kitchen wall of the recently constructed home.

Fortunately, the home was so new that no one lived there yet, but it was also still attended by construction crews that dove out of the way of the spool as it hurtled towards them, and crashed in to the house, coming to rest in the kitchen. The construction crewmen recovered and looked up the two slopes to see where the spool had come from, spotting the two eleven-year old boys, one black, one white peering down with shock filled faces.

One of them yelled, "You two boys come down here right now!" At which point Lee and Bobby looked at each other, and then ran as fast as they could straight home.

We were still the only African-Americans in the whole neighborhood, so after a few inquiries, two representatives from the construction company were standing face to face at our front door with Ruby. They were actually face to chest, because Ruby had reached her maximum adult height and stood four feet eleven inches tall. Surely they were emboldened when they were met by the slight, African-American woman at the door. This would be a mistake.

Ruby had been going to law school at night, and had designs on becoming a lawyer. She had grown up under extreme racist conditions and had developed a feisty disposition. She was not easily intimated. By the time they arrived at our door, she had already plowed into one of her law references and knew all she had to know about "attractive nuisance".

Ruby calmly listened to the men as they smugly attempted to intimidate her. Telling her what damage her son had caused, and that she was responsible for the damage. She waited for them to finish.

Are you gentlemen familiar with the term "attractive nuisance"? she asked. Their response was to look at each other, which told her all she needed to know.

"Let me explain it to you", she continued. "Simply put, it means that a property owner may be held liable for injuries to children trespassing on the property if the injury is caused by an object on the property that is likely to attract children. All of your equipment is easily accessible, and very attractive to every child in this neighborhood. My son is already traumatized over this incident. You are lucky that he was not injured by your negligence. I suggest you spend your efforts securing your equipment, because if something like this happens again, I will sue you. Now get off of my property." The men were never heard from again.

***

When my room in The Jungle evaporated, I didn't even have enough money for a security deposit for an apartment. If not for the generosity of friends and family, I don't know what I would have done. I reached out to everyone I knew, including former coworkers. Many of them had to move out of their comfort zones to find jobs as well. Ollie Matson, one of my teammates from CCSF, had some apartment rooms to rent. He rented one to me, and was lenient on the timeliness of my rent payments. Thank God for real friends.

One of my contacts finally paid off. I had got in touch with a friend from my days at Litton who had landed a job as a manager at Boulevard Dodge in Compton. He hired me as a salesman. I had been educated as an electrical engineer, I had designed circuitry for some of the most advanced aircraft in the world, and I was about to sell used cars. I didn't have time to be ashamed, so I went to work.

There was another plus to this job. Being a car salesman gave me access to a personal car. So I was able to sell the car I had, and send the money to Ruby. Selling cars was all commission. No salary. If I didn't sell, I didn't get paid.

There is an art to selling; if you are too aggressive, you will scare the customer off. Too passive and you never get the deal. You also had to take care of the customer after the sale. If they returned the car during the honeymoon period, my commission would evaporate.

I had sold a used car, to a woman, that had a recurring mechanical problem. The service department kept giving her the runaround. Finally, tiring of the poor service, she decided that she would just return the car. The dealership had sold her a lemon, and she wasn't going to settle for it. I was going to lose my commission.

The woman was a little on the large size, and she had been employed at a fish cannery for the last twenty years. She was using the car to transport her and her equally large friends to and from work every day. Her friends had several years logged at the cannery as well. Over the years the fish smell had worked its way in to the very pores of these women, and when they would sweat, a distinct odor ensued. In the few weeks that she had owned the car, their fish-laden sweat had worked its way in to the cloth seats.

I explained the customer's dissatisfaction with the car to my sales manager, and he relayed it to the owner of the dealership. The owner went to check out the car himself, and when he opened the car door, he was hit in the face with the strong odor of fish. He slammed the door as quickly as he could, grabbed the service man by the arm, and told him in no uncertain terms that he would fix the car to the customer's satisfaction; because there was no way we could ever sell that car to anyone else. My commission was safe.

No matter how good a salesman I was, I couldn't fight the economy. The oil embargo was on, and the economy had cratered. People were not buying cars. Once again, I found myself out of a job. When I lost the car salesman job, I also lost access to a car. No matter how hard I tried, how hard I worked, how well I performed, things just continued to spiral out of my control. I needed money to take care of my family, and I needed a car to go see them. I had neither. In the pecking order of human existence, I was one rung above the homeless. That was only because I had a place to stay.

I had learned to mix drinks and found work as a bartender from time to time. I had also applied with a catering company to tend bar for their events. I didn't have access to a car, but I figured I could get rides around LA when I got called for a job. One afternoon I got a call from the caterer to work a party, but it wasn't in LA, it was in Anaheim which was thirty miles away. The purpose of the party was to celebrate the opening of a new bank office. Because the party was to be held in the bank, there was no bar. As a sub-contracted bartender, I had to bring my own bartending tools. All I had were two pourers and a stirrer. But that wasn't my biggest problem. I still didn't have a car.

I put my bartending tools in a carrying bag with some shoes. Draped some black pants over a coat-hanger and arranged a white shirt around it with the bow tie in the pocket. Then I tucked my wardrobe in to a dry-cleaning bag. It was a hot Southern California day, so I pulled on some shorts and a tee shirt. With my bag in one hand and the clothing bag over my shoulder, I walked out the door. I made my way to the freeway entrance, and stuck out my thumb.

I suppose there is a special kind of look to a forty-four-year-old man hitchhiking while holding a hanger with work clothes. I may have been down on my luck, but I was trying. I wasn't looking for a hand out. I was hustling like I had since I was nine years old.

It wasn't too long before I had a ride. I asked to be let out where the freeways interchange, then I walked down the bank, tossed my bags over the fence and climbed the fence reaching the I-5 to Anaheim.

I shared my story with the next driver to pick me up, and he gave me a much appreciated ride all the way to the bank where the party was being held. I was touched by his generosity. My good fortune continued as one of the other bartenders offered me a ride all the way home after the party.

Hitchhiking became a way of life for me. I had committed to coaching Brian's Pop Warner football team. So I would hitchhike 30 miles from LA to Rowland Heights. I did this two or three days a week. After my visit, Ruby drove me back to the freeway, and I hitchhiked home. The boys never knew. I made Ruby promise not to tell them.

The catering company was pleased with my work, and more work came my way. Hearing my transportation plight, they allowed me to ride in the catering truck if I could make my way to the office before they left for an event. I did this for several months. Eventually, one of the managers from the catering company sold me her '65 Chrysler.

As I struggled to keep my head above water, it helped immensely to see that Skip and Lee were thriving in high school. They had both joined the marching band and were popular athletes. Skip played basketball, and continued to play football, starting at running back his junior and senior years. He was also attracted to gymnastics. He competed on the floor exercise and vaulting events. Lee followed his lead in to the gym and became one of the best in California on the still ring event. Brian was playing Pop Warner football.

As helpless as I felt to change my situation, it paled in comparison to the helplessness I felt when I got the call one late afternoon from the boy's gymnastics coach.

It was January 29, 1973. Skip was at gymnastics practice attempting a new tumbling move. It was a front one and a half forward flip. The move called for him to run three steps, elevate, flip one and a half times in the air, land head first, and roll out of it. He elevated and flipped as required, but landed awkwardly. Skip shook it off, slowly walking back to attempt the move again.

The gymnastics coach, Dave Martin, also doubled as a football coach. He knew Skip well. Knew he was tough. Knew Skip was fearless. Conventional wisdom called for young men to shake off injuries. To get back on the horse. Skip was an accomplished football player. A seventeen-year-old senior, he was the starting running back at Rowland High with designs on playing football in college like I did. He had been hit hard plenty of times.

But Coach Martin was not a conventional coach. So he insisted that practice was over, and Skip was going to the hospital. For that, I will always be grateful because unbeknownst to anyone at the time, Skip had dislocated his C7, and crushed his C6 vertebrae. Skip had broken his neck.

I was 30 miles away when I got the call. It may as well have been 300. I had imperfect information. I knew Skip was in the hospital and that he had injured his neck, but I did not know the extent of the damage. I couldn't get there fast enough. Traffic, parking, registration, room assignment, elevators – were all impediments to me reaching my son.

When I finally reached his room, opened the door and saw him, it was like taking a sucker punch to the gut. I couldn't breathe. A scream welled up inside of me. It took every inch of strength not to burst into tears.

The room smelled of antiseptic. Skip lay on his back in the sterile hospital room. There were small sandbags bracing either side of his head to keep it immobile. The sides of his head were shaved. They had drilled small holes into his skull on both sides. Small steel rods, the size of nails were inserted into the holes. Attached to the rods was a stirrup which allowed the medical team to hang a weight on the end to create tension and keep his spine from collapsing. The whole apparatus resembled something a clandestine agency would use to extract secrets from a spy.

Skip, as all of my boys, was active since he could walk. He was very popular in high school, nominated as Favorite Man on Campus in his senior year. He played trumpet in the marching band, and he sang and played guitar. He discovered gymnastics was a way to leverage his leg strength. He was always one to try new tricks. He could tumble with the best of them. Now I was just hoping he would walk again. The break was not fatal. My fear, as any parent's would be, was that he would have permanent spinal damage and lose the use of his limbs.

I stepped into the room and slowly moved towards him. I wanted to scream "No!!", but I had to show strength – for his sake.

Skip lay awake on the bed. Unable to turn his head, he strained his eyes in my direction to see who had come in to the room. He saw it was me. Seeing the anguish on my face, he did the only thing he could do; he smiled and said, "Don't worry, Dad. I'm going to be OK." That's when the flood gates opened.

12 STAR WARS

Selling used cars, tending bar, selling watches and security windows, hitchhiking to jobs - I thought those things made life tough, but they were nothing compared to what Skip was dealing with. I didn't have the luxury of self-pity.

The prognosis called for the surgeons to drill a plug of bone from his hip and fuse it into his neck. The procedure had certain risks, but we had little choice. If Skip was going to get back to being a healthy young man again, this was the path to take.

I had never felt so helpless. With my predicaments, there was always something I could do. I could look for another job; I could hustle like I had since I was a little boy. But with this, all I could do was hope and pray.

After his neck was fused, he was affixed with a steel halo that connected through brackets to a neck brace. He lay in bed, immobile, for week after week. Unwilling to put pressure on his neck, the doctors would not elevate him. Instead, in order to vary his position, he was strapped to the bed which could then be flipped 180 degrees, like a piece of meat roasting on a spigot. He was out of immediate danger, but only time would tell if the bones would fuse properly, or if there would be any lasting negative effects.

After several weeks of slow recovery, the operation was deemed to be an unqualified success. Skip started the long, slow journey of rehabilitation. I visited as much as I could. Whenever I did, the room was packed with his high school friends and his brothers. It helped immensely to see him surrounded by people to cheer him up. The hospital actually became a great place for kids to hang out.

It wasn't long before he was walking again, and he would make several trips around the floor of the hospital. The steel halo affixed to his head and the neck brace combined to make him look like something out of a horror movie. He took full advantage of that. When he could walk, he took great pleasure in frightening the other patients as he exaggerated a long slow, painful walk in front of their doorways. He would get his laughs at their expense. But he would also go in search of a lonely patient and play guitar for them.

Skip never lost the use of his limbs. Everything worked fine. Of course, he would never play competitive sports again. But Skip never complained about the physical therapy, or how his life had suddenly changed. He ultimately enjoyed a full recovery, with no after affects from the accident. God had been smiling on him that day.

The following year, things slowly began to get better for me as well. After Skip's recovery, Lee received a Congressional nomination to attend West Point. And after almost three years of doing any job that came along, I finally got a job I could hold my head up about. I was hired by Litton for the second time as a design engineer, and shortly after that, I found a better job with Hughes Engineering. Hughes was building satellite tracking equipment, and I became a manager in the manufacturing department. This was my first exposure to the satellite industry. I didn't know it then, but it would set me on a path to be part of a renowned weapons defense development team in the future.

Before I could completely crawl out of my dark place, there was one more punch to the gut I had to endure. My dad, Big Walt, died of pancreatic cancer at the age of seventy-two. This was not the last time pancreatic cancer would cast its shadow on our family.

The saying goes that it is always easier to get a job when you already have a job. Once established at Hughes, my credibility was restored, and an old friend recruited me for an engineering sales position at Raytheon. I worked at Raytheon for three years, and then leveraged that into an opportunity with the government, starting as a GS-11 logistics manager. I was hired into the Naval Air Systems Command (NAVAIR) in Point Mugu Naval Air Station in California.

NAVAIR's mission was to provide full life-cycle support of naval aviation aircraft, weapons, and systems operated by sailors and marines. At Point Mugu, the military tested and tracked weapons systems in restricted air and sea space. I was providing logistics on the F-14 Tomcat fighter aircraft and the Tomahawk missile. I was back in my element. My success or failure was going to be a function of how I performed. I had been to hell and back. I would work as hard as I always had, and I would be rewarded for my performance. That's the way the world worked, and I was overdue. I was working for a black manager, so I knew race was not going to be a hindrance to my advancement. I was soon positioned for a promotion to GS-12. But there was just one thing I hadn't counted on – an itch I couldn't scratch for my supervisor. He was saving the spot that I should have been promoted to for a subordinate he was trying to bed. I couldn't compete with that. There were lots of things I would do for a job. I had to draw the line somewhere.

I had a fraternity brother working at Port Hueneme who said that he could get me to a GS-12 if I interviewed well. I did, and was promoted to GS-12 in the Ship Design and Support Division. It was there that I expanded my knowledge and experience as a logistician. Logisticians were responsible for getting the right equipment, in the right place, at the right time and cost. They were the life blood of the military. My area of focus was electronic components. I could apply my technical experience to the supply chain. We were supporting Naval Sea Systems Command (NAVSEA) in Washington working on the DDG-963 destroyers. Those became the first guided missile cruisers in the navy, and a precursor to the CG-47, which I would work on later. I was in constant communication with senior naval officers there, and had developed a strong rapport with Jack Hargrove, a GS-14. After three years of meeting and exceeding their requests, Jack asked that I relocate to Washington to join his group. To sweeten the offer, he assured me that I would be promoted to GS-13. Ranks of GS-13, 14, and 15 were referred to as GS-Magnificents. A GS-13 is equivalent to a commander in the navy and a lieutenant colonel in the army.

I was looking forward to my promotion. I didn't receive it upon arrival. I knew I needed to establish myself, prove myself first. I continued to expand my scope as a logistics manager for NAVSEA in Washington. As the logistics manager, my job was to ensure that when cruisers launched, they were equipped with all required electronic components for weapons systems and navigation. Most importantly, the components were installed in such a way that they would continue to function under combat conditions. The method the navy used to test reliability under fire was to conduct shock trials. A shock trial consists of detonating hundreds of pounds of explosives in close proximity to the ship, putting the entire ship under extreme duress. Typically, 18% to 20% of the equipment would become inoperable at the conclusion of these tests. As a former sailor, and sonar technician, I understood firsthand the importance of reliable equipment in a combat zone.

My first shock trial was to be held near Cape Canaveral, Florida. My team flew down and was treated to a view of a satellite launch before the trials began.

We had loaded a ship with 500 units of highly sensitive electronic equipment – the nervous system for navigation and weapons. The trial was conducted off-shore with explosion after explosion rocking the ship. The results would not be known for several hours while audit crews tested all of the equipment to see if we performed at least as well as the 18% to 20% fail rate. Some failure was always expected, and crews needed to be able to understand how to adapt in combat. It was important to know what components were most susceptible to failure.

Me and my team retired to a local watering hole to wait out the results. That's where the supporting officer found us to deliver the news.

"Walt the results are in." His face gave away nothing. "I'm pleased to inform you that not one piece of equipment failed the shock trial on either ship. You and your team produced results with 100% reliability." The shock trial wasn't supposed to shock me, but it accomplished just that. We had achieved a 100% success rate. Not one electrical component on the ship that I was accountable for failed. The rest of the night was a blur as we celebrated.

That was just the beginning of a string of successful results for me and my team. Now we had the recipe. Over the next four years as chief logistics manager, we launched five ships, and survived the shock trials with 100% reliability on all five ships. I was receiving outstanding reviews and recognition. With that kind of record, the promotion to GS-13 that I had been promised was surely mine. But year after year, for four years, no matter how I performed, the promotion never came. My supervisor continued to bring people in over me. I had established myself as one of the best, if not the best logistician the group had ever seen, but my career was being stymied.

I had befriended one of the senior administrative assistants there who always had an ear to the ground. She had heard the discussions with my boss and our other senior managers. She kept telling me,

"Walt, they are never going to promote you." After four years, I finally believed her. I had had enough.

They wouldn't promote me, but they continued to give me rave reviews. I packaged up my resume along with my reviews and began to shop around. I still had my engineering credentials, and I had a friend who was the assistant secretary of the navy, Fred Davidson, that I had confided in. He said, "Walt, I'm tired of hearing how they are jerking you around. I can get you transferred to engineering, and promoted to GS-13 right away." So I submitted my transfer papers and waited for approval to transfer. But the approvals never came.

The military is usually pretty good at recognizing good performance. The motivational value of doing so has been ingrained in the US military for a long time. The performance of me and my team had not gone unnoticed, so when my transfer request hit the desk of the commanding admiral, Admiral Wayne E. Meyer, all hell broke loose. Seated between myself and Admiral Meyer in the pecking order was my boss, a GS-14, his boss, a GS-15, and a navy captain. He called all three of them in to his office and demanded to know why Walt Jourdan was transferring out of his division. When they told him it was because I was long overdue a promotion, he cursed them out, and ordered that I be promoted immediately. I was in my office, with my resume and performance history in hand, preparing to head over to the Pentagon looking for more job prospects, when I felt a hand on my shoulder. It was my boss with my promotion papers, congratulating me on my promotion to GS-13.

I thanked him, and accepted the promotion, but the damage had already been done. The last four years had left a bad taste in my mouth. My supervisor was still going to be there, and the environment would not be a positive one. I floated my resume to a few other divisions, and was offered a GS-13.5 from the CIA – which was basically a GS-13 with a bump in salary. I declined, as I knew I was good enough for a GS-14. That persistence paid off.

I kept my eyes open for other prospects. My success as a logistician had also caught the attention of the Defense Nuclear Agency, which had an opening at GS-14 for a logistics manager. It was a Thursday afternoon when I sat down with the hiring manager. Halfway through the interview, he came around from his desk, sat down next to me, put his hand on my arm, and talked about the things that we were going to accomplish together. I knew I had the job.

The following Tuesday I received the official offer. Not only was I about to be promoted to GS-14 just ten months after being promoted to GS-13, but I would be working on America's nuclear defense team. We would be designing the ultimate nuclear defense system.

I was vetted for a top secret clearance by the NSA, and began my new assignment. This was the culmination of my foundation as a design engineer and my success as a logistics manager. My new colleagues would never guess that, just a few years prior, I had been standing on the side of the road, hitchhiking my way to a bartending gig, or selling used cars to put food on the table. I had finally climbed all the way out of that dark hole.

Of course, Washington DC wasn't all work and no play. My old college roommate, Burl Toler, had established himself as an official in the NFL. Officials were privy to a set of four complimentary tickets to whichever games they were officiating each week. When Burl came to DC, I was often the recipient of those complimentary tickets. They were always good seats, so I had an opportunity to treat my friends to a Redskins game.

Ruby and I had been divorced for more than a decade, and it was not unusual for me to bring someone to the game who I was seeing at the time.

On this particular Sunday, the Dallas Cowboys were in town. Burl knew they were my favorite team, he was able to give me three nice seats. The fourth, he said, he had to give to another friend that he owed a favor to. Knowing I would bring a girlfriend, he asked if she might have another girlfriend of hers to bring along. I thought this was odd, as Burl was not the kind of guy to ask me to bring a friend along for him. But I didn't question it. The tickets he gave me were for seats 8, 9, and 11. He said we could just re-arrange the seats at the game.

I showed up to the game with my grateful friends in tow, looking forward to a great afternoon. We slid down the row to our three seats, when the person sitting in the fourth seat came in to focus.

It was none other than my ex-wife, Ruby. She happened to be in town for business, and Burl gave her the fourth ticket to the game. He had set me up. He just knew that I would be escorting two lady-friends, and wanted to put me in the pressure-cooker, sitting right next to my ex-wife.

The officials hadn't taken the field yet, but I could just picture Burl somewhere in the bowels of the stadium, laughing his ass off.

What Burl hadn't counted on was that I had male friends too, and I had brought along just one woman, and a buddy of mine. So, I didn't come across as the playboy he figured me for.

The four of us ended up having a great time, and Ruby even joined us at my place after the game for a couple glasses of wine. We talked about how our lives had evolved, and she was thrilled to hear about my new job.

The level of technology I would be working with

in the Nuclear Defense Agency was truly state of the art. The vision was to create an umbrella of satellite-mounted protection to stave off a nuclear attack. This technology would be capable of imparting enough energy into a small object that it could accelerate from zero to 7,000 mph over a distance of only fourteen feet. It was the beginning of what would later be called a rail gun. I was responsible for logistics: making sure we had the resources and equipment we needed, when we needed it, and that it met the highest standards required for national defense. It was the cornerstone of the administration's vision for nuclear defense. It was dubbed "Star Wars" by the media, and its sponsor was Ronald Reagan. A man that I greatly admired, and had already met.

* * *

A few years earlier, in 1982, when I was working for NAVSEA in the State Department, I had connected with a Kappa Alpha Psi fraternity brother of mine, named Donald Delandro. Don was a brigadier general in the army, and the first Black adjutant general of the US Army. He was also originally from New Orleans, as I was. Don introduced me to Steve Rhodes. Steve, another high ranking Black civil servant, had been appointed by President Reagan to serve in the White House

Office of Intergovernmental Affairs as special assistant liaison to city and county officials. Steve was also from New Orleans, and he and I became fast friends. Steve invited me quite regularly to the White House for lunch. I already carried top secret clearance from my position with NAVAIR, so access was not a problem. The White House lunch hall, just across from the White House was a special treat.

Steve had a keen interest in seeing that Reverend Martin Luther King, Jr's birthday became a national holiday, and had heard through White House gossip that the president had changed his mind and would not sign the bill. Steve confided in me that he would resign his position if that was the case. He shared this gossip with Vice President Bush who took him by the hand to the Oval Office and was asked to repeat what he had heard to the president. The president let out a few expletives and repeated in plain language that he would indeed be signing the bill.

Shortly afterwards, President Reagan hosted an MLK birthday dinner. Steve had arranged for me to attend. I was beside myself, and reminisced about sitting on my father's shoulders as a boy, waiving at FDR.

The dinner was well attended, so I had no expectations of actually meeting the president. I was just thrilled to be at the White House, and to be in the presence of a sitting president. If only my father could see me now.

The White House was packed with dignitaries including Congressman Jack Kemp, Senator Bob Dole, and Mrs. Coretta Scott King. At the conclusion of the dinner, it became clear that it wasn't just a dinner to celebrate the great man's birthday, but a day to announce that, from this day forth, all American's would celebrate this day. At the conclusion of the dinner, the president announced that he had made the decision to make MLK's birthday a national holiday.

It was a day I will always remember, and a day that I could take stock in how far I had come. Not just recovering from the recession that tested my resolve, but from my time as a young boy, helping my family through tough times.

To my gratification, there was indeed a reception line that night. The president and First Lady were going to greet each one of us. I found my place in line and moved forward, thinking back through my path to where I currently stood. As I approached the president, his aide-de-camp whispered my name and my position in the president's ear. President Reagan looked me in the eye, and gave me a firm grip. "Welcome to the White House, Mr. Jourdan."

"It's an honor, Mr. President."

What he saw was a senior logistics manager from the State Department. But if he peeled back the layers, he would find a technical sales engineer, father, watch salesman, window security salesman, used car salesman, bartender, coach, aviation design engineer, electrical engineer, delivery man, navy sonar technician, national football champion, boxer, enforcer, numbers runner, and of course... shoeshine boy.

13 EPILOGUE

After almost seven years in Washington, culminating with my work on Star Wars, I was ready to head back home to California to work for the government in the area of logistics. There, out of all the armed forces in Northern California, I received the manager of the year award. A few years later, the base where I worked was closed, and I went to work for the Bureau of Reclamation as Superintendent in the Tracy, California office. The only Black Superintendent at the time, I again achieved manager of the year honors. Finally, I found my way back to work in the defense industry as a Marketing Executive for ManTech, a contractor specializing in national security. Before I retired, I made peace with Hawaii and in 1991 returned there on vacation. I retired to Las Vegas in 2001.

My youngest son, Brian, went on to own and operate a couple of small businesses before obtaining his commercial driver's license and become an independent contractor in the transportation sector. He currently works in the construction industry. Unmarried at the time of writing, he continues to enjoy the bachelor life and has settled in Portland, Oregon.

Leland (Lee) graduated from West Point, received an honorable discharge from the US Army as a Captain, and became a Vice President in one of Chevron's international business units. Married for 35 years to Diane, Lee has three children: Byron, Leland II (known as TJ), and Halle. Halle earned her undergraduate degree from Central Washington University in social sciences with a concentration in psychology, and works in the health industry. TJ, while earning a Batchelor of Arts degree, has earned credit as a screenwriter on two feature-length motion pictures, and is a scratch golfer. Byron and his wife, Julie, who is a registered nurse at a level 1 Trauma hospital in the medical cardiac Intensive Care Unit, gave me my first great-grandchild, a girl named Payton, and my first great-grandson, Miles. After graduating from the University of Texas, Byron became a group manager with Microsoft, and later, continuing the legacy of Jourdan's at Honeywell, became senior manager of Go To Market Strategy at Honeywell.

Walter (Skip), while working as a flight attended for United Airlines, co-founded a software business that has earned a US Patent and provides online route scheduling services for United, Continental, and Southwest flight crews. This business continues to have success after more than two decades. Married to Mona, who is a registered nurse in a Neonatal Intensive Care Unit, they have two daughters. The eldest is Princess, a business graduate of Georgetown University who worked for the Peace Corps for over two years in Ethiopia, and currently applies her security clearance working for the Office of the Inspector General. She and her husband, Wasihun, gave me my second great-grandson, Jonah. Skip's second daughter, Maya, is a sophomore at the University of Nevada, Reno, studying Kinesiology.

Ruby stayed in Rowland Heights until 1975, and then moved to North Hollywood. After a long teaching career, she got back to computer programming, first working in the energy industry and then moving to Arlington Virginia to work for the government. She was engaged to re-marry in 1994, but sadly, was diagnosed with pancreatic cancer. She passed away the same year she was diagnosed. I had remained close to her family and attended her funeral in Portland. Her younger sisters, Joy and Beverly still live in Portland. Joy contributed to this book. In 1966, Asa and Letitia Brock, Ruby's parents, were honored as Family of the Year by the Urban league of Portland. The annual award is made to parents who have overcome obstacles and achieved success in raising a family through hard work and determination. Asa retired from Union Pacific the following year, after forty-three years of service. He was stricken with cancer, and passed away February 8 1980, at the age of seventy-eight. Letitia passed away on January 12, 2002 at the age of one hundred and one.

Before I left Washington, I was invited to the White House for one more major event: Ronald Reagan's signing of MLK's birthday as a national holiday. I sat in the second row and took several pictures to commemorate the event. One of those pictures I converted into a commemorative poster. The Republican National Committee has purchased over 600 copies of my poster.

In 2010, I was diagnosed with lymphoma. By the grace of God, and the support of friends and family, it is in remission. I am an active member of the North Las Vegas Rotary, the Kappa Alpha Psi fraternity, the Lions Club, and the Remnant Ministries Church, whose pastor is the former NFL quarterback, Randall Cunningham.

Walter Thomas Jourdan, Dad, "Big Walt"

Jennie Jourdan, Mom

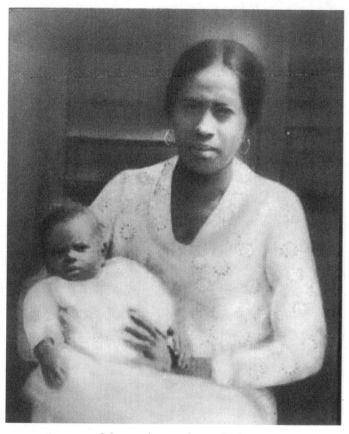

My mother and me, 1929

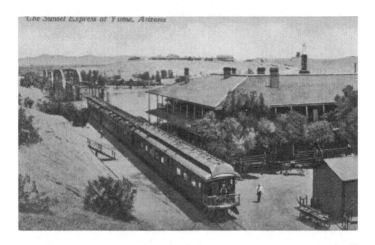

The Sunset Express at Yuma, Arizona

The Sunset Express New Orleans to San Francisco
circa 1930s

(Newman Post Card Co. San Francisco)

Big Walt and Uncle Spencer

We rented two bedrooms in the upper floor of this house on 36th Street in Oakland, California from 1930 to 1933. Nine of us lived here at one time.

University High School, Oakland, California

City College San Francisco National Champions
1948. I am number 27.

Me (left) and Ollie Matson (center) hanging out at the Student Lounge, 1948.

Jughead (left), and Me at San Francisco State College, 1950.

Ray Urbano

Some modeling in my 20s

DE 667 USS Wiseman

(Photo credit Navsource.org)

Me and Ruby – the night we left for Portland to get married, December 1953.

Ruby, two months pregnant with Skip, 1955.

Our first home. Stanley Avenue, Los Angeles,
1961.

My three sons. Skip (left), Lee (right), Brian (front), 1964.

Ruby the glamour queen

Both Ruby and I contributed to the development of
the X-15

Our Home in Rowland Heights, California, 1966.

'65 Chrysler – no more hitchhiking

Colleagues at Litton 1975

Naval Shock trial

Manager of the year, 1980s

Ruby's parents, Asa and Letitia Brock

Meeting Bruce Jenner

Meeting Lynn Swann and John Robinson

Meeting President Ronald Reagan and First Lady,
Nancy Reagan at the White House

My photo of Reagan signing the Bill, making MLK birthday a Holiday. My friend, Steve Rhodes, is standing second from the right.

Burl Toler and Daughter, Susan Toler Carr.

(Photo by Darrell Carr)

Randall Cunningham (left) with Brian

Lee's family

Me with Skip's family

Burl Toler (center standing), me (right), and Ollie Matson (seated)

Bibliography

1. Sunset Limited, Wikipedia
   https://en.wikipedia.org/wiki/Sunset_Limited
   Accessed November 3, 2015
2. The phrase finder, Running Numbers
   http://www.phrases.org.uk/bulletin_board/5/me
   ssages/1485.html
   Accessed November 10, 2016
3. Treasure Island, San Francisco Wikipedia
   https://en.wikipedia.org/wiki/Treasure_Island,_
   San_Francisco
   Accessed December 5, 2015
4. Japanese-American Internment Camps
   http://www.ht-
   la.org/htla/projects/oralhistory/japaneseinternm
   ent/timeline.html
   Accessed December 15, 2015
5. Harry S. Truman Library & Museum
   http://www.trumanlibrary.org/whistlestop/study
   _collections/desegregation/large/index.php?acti
   on=bg
   Accessed September 15,2016
6. Naval History and Heritage Command.
   http://www.history.navy.mil.
   Accessed November 11, 2015

7. U.S. Naval Operations during the Korean War.
    http://www.nj.gov/military/korea/factsheets/nav
    y.html.
    Accessed October 12, 2015
8. U.S.S. Hanna (DE-449), Wikipedia.
    https://en.wikipedia.org/wiki/USS_Hanna_(DE
    -449).
    Accessed January 4, 2016
9. Tide Times for Inch'on, Tide Forecast.
    http://www.tide-forecast.com/locations/Inchon-
    South-Korea/tides/latest.
    Accessed October 15, 2016
10. U.S. Military Causalities of War, Wikipedia.
    https://en.wikipedia.org/wiki/United_States_mi
    litary_casualties_of_war.
    Accessed February 2, 2016
11. North American Aviation (NAA), Wikipedia.
    https://en.wikipedia.org/wiki/North_American_
    Aviation.
    Accessed March 2, 2016
12. North American X-15, Wikipedia.
    https://en.wikipedia.org/wiki/North_American_
    X-15.
    Accessed March 13, 2016
13. NAVAIR, U.S. Navy Naval Air Systems
    Command.
    http://www.navair.navy.mil/index.cfm.
    Accessed April 9, 2016

14. Black Exclusion Laws in Oregon, The Oregon Encyclopaedia.
    https://oregonencyclopedia.org/articles/exclusion_laws/#.V9YAAWf2Zes.
    Accessed April 5, 2016

15. ESPN
    http://www.espn.com/nfl/news/story?id=4405963
    Accessed September 12, 2016

16. Cover art by Jia Sung

Made in the USA
San Bernardino, CA
06 December 2016